PRAISE FOR LAUREN AND TONY DUNGY'S BOOKS

"With a 'he said/she said' format, former NFL coach Dungy (*Quiet Strength*) and his wife, Lauren, share lessons learned over more than thirty years of marriage. They are different in personality, but their deep faith and commitment to their relationship help them grow closer through career changes, multiple moves, the rearing of nine children, and family tragedy. They discuss the wide variety of incidents and factors that have strengthened their marriage, like working through different communication styles and learning the importance of praying together. They also share the difficulties through which they have walked together, like being in the public eye—Tony became the first African-American head coach to guide a team to the Super Bowl—dealing with the loss of a parent; and coping with the suicide of their son. They offer their thoughts in personal, conversational style with the hope that readers can recognize some part of their own marriage and be able to find guidance, hope, and encouragement. The book reads more like an enjoyable chat with longtime friends than the helpful marriage guidebook that it is."

    PUBLISHERS WEEKLY on *Uncommon Marriage*

"Tony Dungy's life is a living testimony of a man's faith in God. He has given us a new picture and definition of a Coach. Good guys do come in first!"

    LOVIE SMITH, head coach of the Houston Texans

"In this fast-paced American culture with so many people driven by the lure of material success, Tony Dungy reminds us what truly matters in the game of life. At the pinnacle of NFL success, he has taken time to show us the value of making memories and not just money, focusing on family instead of fame, and building up a storehouse of eternal wealth that can never be depleted. Don't just read this book; 'listen' to it with the ears of your soul."

PRISCILLA SHIRER, author and speaker, on *Quiet Strength*

"In today's world, where sports figures and movie stars are idolized, Tony Dungy is a true hero because his life is a testimony to the fact that if you 'do your best and let God do the rest,' not only will success follow, but your life will have a positive impact on others. This is the reason I consider Tony a great friend and role model."

BENJAMIN S. CARSON SR., MD, former professor and director of pediatric neurosurgery, Johns Hopkins Medical Institutes

"My good friend Tony Dungy has demonstrated in his personal life and in this powerful book that it is possible to be a committed Christian on and off the field and still come out a winner. This insightful work will challenge, encourage, and inspire all who read it to uncompromisingly integrate our faith into every aspect of our lives, so that we, too, will be victorious in spite of the challenges and obstacles that life brings our way."

TONY EVANS, senior pastor, Oak Cliff Bible Fellowship; president, The Urban Alternative, on *Quiet Strength*

"Amid the deafening roar surrounding the machinery of earthly glory, the spiritual man leaves quiet footsteps of inspired faith. Tony Dungy's footprints can be traced back to God and family. This foundation has provided him with the love, strength, compassion, and tolerance to fill his earthly run with man's greatest gift and purpose . . . to be of service to God and his fellow man."

JIM IRSAY, owner of the Indianapolis Colts

"In the twenty-one years that I've known Tony Dungy, I have consistently found him to be a man of integrity, sincerity, and openness. As a man of faith, no matter what trials or tribulations he's faced, he has embodied the Scripture found in Proverbs 16:32: 'He that is slow to anger is better than the mighty; and he that ruleth his spirit than he that taketh a city.' Dungy has followed the biblical prescription for success. In football and in the game of life, Tony Dungy is a winner."

JAMES BROWN, host of *The NFL Today* on CBS Sports

"Tony Dungy is a world champion in every way. His quiet strength both on and off the field has been an inspiration to millions. His sense of priority is uncommon and uncompromised. His purposeful desire to turn the spotlight off himself and on to Christ is admirable. Even more impressive, however, is the character and dignity he exemplifies when there are no cameras . . . when there is no spotlight. This is a man of tremendous faith, and he lives it every day of his life. He has inspired me, and I'm so thankful for his friendship."

MICHAEL W. SMITH, vocalist and songwriter

"For over a decade, Tony Dungy has quietly taught me significant lessons in leadership and in life. Now he's sharing them with you in this thought-provoking book. In *Quiet Strength*, Tony leads us on a journey that reveals profound principles for living and our ultimate purpose in life."

MARK W. MERRILL, president, Family First and All Pro Dad

UNCOMMON INFLUENCE

LAUREN & TONY DUNGY

Foreword by Santiago "Jimmy" Mellado, president and CEO of Compassion International

UNCOMMON

SAYING YES TO A PURPOSEFUL LIFE

INFLUENCE

Tyndale House Publishers
Carol Stream, Illinois

Visit Tyndale online at tyndale.com.

Visit the Dungy Family Foundation online at dungyfamilyfoundation.org.

TYNDALE and Tyndale's quill logo are registered trademarks of Tyndale House Ministries.

Uncommon Influence: Saying Yes to a Purposeful Life

Designed by Julie Chen

Published in association with the literary agency of Legacy, LLC, Winter Park, Florida 32789.

For information about special discounts for bulk purchases, please contact Tyndale House Publishers at csresponse@tyndale.com, or call 1-800-323-9400.

Library of Congress Cataloging-in-Publication Data

A catalog record for this book is available from the Library of Congress.

ISBN 978-1-4964-5889-6

Printed in the United States of America

28 27 26 25 24 23 22
7   6   5   4   3   2   1

For Lauren's late mother, Doris J. "Bird" Harris.
Her unselfish love and commitment to Kingdom-building
provided a beautiful model for us to follow.

CONTENTS

FOREWORD

As a kid, one of my heroes was the late Tom Landry, legendary head coach of the Dallas Cowboys football team from 1960 to 1988. He led his team to two Super Bowl victories during his time in Dallas and coached his teams to twenty consecutive winning seasons—a staggering record that stands to this day. I grew up in the late 1960s and early 1970s as Coach Landry was setting records and leaving his mark, and I remember the impression that was left on me as I watched him work while living out his faith through it all. I wasn't watching him from a neighboring community or a residence a few states away; I was watching him from my childhood homes in Managua, Nicaragua, and later, Panama City, Panama. And while my genetic makeup meant I'd never play in the NFL, I suspected that if I could apply the same discipline, balance, character, and faithfulness to Jesus to my efforts that it seemed Coach Landry applied to his, perhaps I could be a force for good in life like he was. I so admired him that I wrote him a letter when I was in the sixth grade and was shocked when I received a personally signed response. I cherished that piece of paper for years and have kept it to this day.

I never had the privilege of meeting Tom Landry in person, but to this day I consider him an early mentor of mine. He shaped my thinking and my priorities during that pivotal period in every adolescent's life—when a child is figuring out what kind of adult to be.

Around the same time that I was making my way to the States to attend college at Southern Methodist University—on scholarship for track and field, as it would turn out—a man named Tony Dungy was beginning his coaching career, working first with his alma mater, the University of Minnesota, and eventually with the Pittsburgh Steelers, where he'd played for two years. Not long after I graduated from college, Tony made sports headlines by being named the youngest defensive coordinator in the league. He'd go on to coach the Kansas City Chiefs and the Minnesota Vikings before becoming a head coach—first with the Tampa Bay Buccaneers and then, of course, with the Indianapolis Colts, where he'd net a Super Bowl win. From time to time, I'd catch media interviews with Tony, and whenever I heard him speak, I'd think about how familiar his approach sounded to me. I'd later learn that Coach Landry had been a hero of Tony's, too, and that according to Tony the reason he'd succeeded in the sport was because of those Landry-esque principles we'd both esteemed.

Discipline.

Life balance.

Character.

Faithfulness to Jesus.

In 2010 I was thrilled to meet Tony in person, after he accepted my invitation to speak at a conference for pastors and leaders I helped organize each year. By then I'd begun watching him carefully: How did he handle victory? How did he handle defeat? How did he handle personal adversity? Over time, would the pressures of coaching make him snap or change him in a bad way? What I discovered filled me with respect and admiration.

Through the inevitable ups and downs of life, it seemed nothing could take him off course. Tony Dungy really was *that* consistently measured, *that* committed to living a life of integrity, *that* energized by serving others, and *that* encouraging of everyone he met. It was obvious that he valued helping young athletes navigate the challenges of early stardom. And that he enjoyed speaking into the lives of other coaches, of other dads, of people who were incarcerated, of anyone God put in his path. And that he longed to learn more and more about his faith. And that he was committed to getting sharper, more skilled, himself.

These things all remain true of Tony today. But while he might give the NFL's finest—Coach Landry, of course, but also Tony's beloved first boss, Coach Chuck Noll—credit for envisioning him in his role as a football coach, he'd tell you that the person who first inspired him to live beyond himself in any kind of fully orbed way was his wise and winsome wife, Lauren. It was on the day when she said, "Tony, I think we should adopt."

. . .

For the thirty-nine years of their marriage, Lauren and Tony Dungy have operated as a dream team, working relentlessly on behalf of those who are marginalized, oppressed, and caught in the crosshairs of others' poor choices. As someone who grew up in less-than-lavish circumstances and who now fights daily to release children from poverty in Jesus' name, I am never more impressed than when I see people of status and means choose *joyfully* to invest themselves in lifting others up. Early on, Lauren and Tony traded the goals of fame, fortune, and the world's flawed definition of success for the goals of inspiring those who were downcast by including them and loving them well. This life strategy is what led them to become pillars in their community, to be seen as a crucial part of their local church, and to reflect the love of Jesus to so many adopted children.

What a win for those precious children.

What a win for Lauren and Tony.

What a win for us *all*. Goodness begets goodness. Our world could use a bit more goodness, I think.

To the casual observer, it may seem as though Lauren and Tony are just "that type of people," the type that is magically wired from birth to be helpful and kind. But this couldn't be further from the truth. The Dungys' style of living was born of thoughtfulness, commitment, and faith. They didn't stumble into significance; they *fought* their way to this aim. And with this book, we get an inside look at how that unfolded and an opportunity to learn from their example of how to become the goodness we need.

Several years ago, I came across a stat in a book I was reading that said a full *95 percent* of our behaviors as human beings are dictated by the inertia of what we've done in the past—the habits we've formed over time.[1] Ninety-five percent! Far less of our lives is driven by individual, thoughtfully processed

---

[1] The book I was reading was David and Caron Loveless's *Nothing to Prove* (CreateSpace, 2016), and the Lovelesses were citing the work of Dr. Roy Baumeister, who wrote on the topic both in the 1998 edition of the *Journal of Personality and Social Psychology* and in the book he coauthored with John Tierney titled, *Willpower: Why Self-Control Is the Secret to Success* (Penguin Books, 2011).

choices than I wanted to believe. The rhythms of life that we choose turn into patterns and habits that have incredible consequences—for good or bad.

I kept thinking about that stat as I read an early copy of Lauren and Tony's book, which is when this thought occurred to me: if I focus today's attention on choosing wisely and do the same tomorrow and the day after that, eventually the habit that will inform my behavior will be a good habit—a habit that helps me move toward a good life instead of one that threatens to take me and others down.

Lauren and Tony knew their own hearts well enough to know that if they relied solely on willpower in the moment, they'd never live the life they were called to live. Sure, at any given crossroads they'd *want* to do the right thing. But like you and me and every other person alive, their actions would eventually fail to live up to their noble desires, and the chasm between the two would grow. To solve this problem, they decided to practice the things that mattered most to them so positive habits would start to form life-giving patterns. They searched the Scriptures. They had countless conversations with each other. They invited input from people who had their best interest at heart. They read. They listened. They learned. They prayed. They short-listed their ideals. And then they got busy habituating toward that better life they dreamed of.

The fruit of all that labor is reflected in what you're now holding in your hands. And what I can tell you unequivocally is that as you begin to elevate the eleven practices they've laid out in the chapters to come, your reflexive reaction to the way your life unfolds will get an unmistakable boost. When we start prioritizing things like preparation and teamwork and integrity and prayer, we become the people we long to be. What's more, we *rewire our default pattern*, making it easier to be that way again. In this manner, we remove the daily burden of deciding how to show up in the world. We'll have "pre-decided" our character; now all that's left is to *live*.

There's a line in the pages you're about to read that is one of the best value propositions imaginable, and it says this: "Right living is a *relief*."

Little in this world feels better than experiencing a *relief*. When you've been shouldering a burden or dealing with chronic pain or trying unsuccessfully to untangle a relational knot, nothing is better than knowing relief. You may even be audibly exhaling right now, just reading the word *relief*.

We want life to be *easier*, not harder. We want to do things that *make life work*.

Here's what I want you to know: relief is yours for the taking. And goodness, too. You can choose to experience relief. You can practice things today that will inform all your tomorrows so that those tomorrows are productive and good. Regardless of the choices you've made before, you can choose wisely now. Rack up enough of those choose-wisely days, and before you know it a habit will form. You'll be living a life of impact, and you'll be leaving a legacy that's strong. As is so clearly the case with Lauren and Tony, your influence will be uncommon too.

Santiago "Jimmy" Mellado
President and CEO, Compassion International
Colorado Springs, February 2022

INTRODUCTION

"How Many Kids Do You Have?"

Lauren

This isn't true for every family, I understand, but when my cell phone lights up in the middle of the night, Tony and I are pretty sure we know why. Over the past four decades, we have received somewhere between forty and fifty of these calls, and nearly every time, the person on the other end of the line was asking if we could take in a child in need of care.

I'm not a professional researcher, but based on what my husband and I have seen firsthand, people who are going to make poor decisions generally make those decisions at night—*late* at night. Call it decision fatigue or overloaded self-control or any of a half dozen other phrases that psychologists are prone to use—regardless, what it equates to is a troubled soul finding still *more* trouble once the sun goes down. Hours later, that person then heads home, is confronted by a loved one—"Where have *you* been?"—and things escalate from there. The kids who were fast asleep are now wide-awake and petrified, wondering why the adults in the house are screaming, why one (or both) of those adults is slurring their words or is stoned out of their mind, and why the people who are supposed to be taking care of them can't even take care of themselves.

Police are nearly always called to the home. Sometimes, grandparents or neighbors are involved. Usually, child services shows up. And then we get the call. A stepping-stone of safety—that's how we've come to think of those middle-of-the-night interventions. Tony and the kids and I provide a few days (or weeks or months) of peace and security for a little one whose environment is turbulent at best.

These were the circumstances a few months ago when Dontae and Kallie arrived. It was ten, maybe ten-thirty on a school night, and Tony and I were about to turn off the news and head to bed when my phone lighted up. The agency had a four-year-old boy and his six-month-old sister in their care and wondered if we could take them in.

"It's a bad situation," the agent explained to me. "The extended family member who had custody fell on hard times and returned the boy and his sister to their mom's house, where the mom was living with her boyfriend, who is the baby's father but not the little boy's."

The problem with that turn of events was that the mom and her boyfriend were in an abusive relationship, and while they'd evidently never physically harmed the children, it was no doubt an undesirable place for those kids to be. When I asked how the agency had become involved, the woman on the line said, "A neighbor saw the family member drop off the kids earlier tonight and knew that the mom and her boyfriend weren't even home. Can you imagine? A four-year-old and a six-month-old, home alone?"

The neighbor had called the police, and now these kids had no place to go.

"Absolutely," I said, barely even glancing at Tony, who was searching my face for details. "Bring them here."

"How many?" Tony asked nonchalantly, after I'd ended the call.

"Two," I replied, to which he said with classic calmness and an easy smile, "All right. We'd better get ready, then."

The addition would raise our official kid count to thirteen. The speed at which that number shifted from week to week explains why whenever Tony and I are asked how many kids we have, we need to pause and think. "Well," I tend to say with a good-natured laugh, "it depends on how you want to define the word *have*."

Last Christmas, during a video interview, Dan Patrick asked Tony how many stockings were hanging on the fireplace there in our home, clearly incredulous over the sheer number of them. It took my husband a good six seconds to sort out how many kids we had just then.

"There should be . . . twelve?" he finally ventured. "Yeah, yeah, twelve," he continued, his confidence building. "Lauren, me, ten kids right now."

The operative phrase, of course, being "right now."

. . .

Every so often, I'll flash back in my mind's eye to a service at Bethany Baptist Church in Pittsburgh, which Tony and

I were part of several decades ago, years before we started a family of our own. Our pastor was our beloved friend Richard Allen Farmer, a dedicated believer who refused to settle for a theoretical faith where "trusting Christ" equated to little more than punching a ticket for heaven and then living any way you pleased here on earth. Instead, he chose—both then and still today—to work out his devotion to Jesus in practical, tangible ways, explaining to our congregation that the essence of being Christian was to *actually be like Christ*. The concept of asking, "What would Jesus do?" was far from a trendy slogan to Pastor Farmer, even as the "WWJD" merchandising tour de force was about to be all the rage. He asked himself that question all the time—genuinely, moment by moment, day by day—and then rearranged his thoughts, his habits, his life according to the answers he found.

"We function in the earth by doing what God would do if He were here in the flesh," he would tell us. "We bind, we loose, we proclaim, we alleviate suffering, we encourage, we admonish, we rebuke, we love, we serve."[1]

Pastor Farmer would joke that we were to live like God's body doubles, doing all the stunt work in the world while letting our heavenly Father get all the glory. It was a compelling vision for Tony and me. It was a compelling vision for us all.

From time to time, Pastor Farmer would host guest speakers who embodied this others-centric lifestyle he himself prized, and on one of those Sunday mornings, the topic was caring for children in need. The speaker was with a group called One Church One Child—to search for them today is to find active and fruitful branches still humming along in seven key states. The invitation to those of us sitting in the crowd that day was to live beyond ourselves, to make our lives matter by investing in the lives of little ones in our midst. Tony and I were so moved by the presenter's passion for children, his explanation of the need there in Allegheny County, his determination to solve the problem of kids not having a place to call home, and his boldness in calling believers to get involved—*now*—that as soon as Pastor Farmer dismissed the congregation, we beelined it for the information table at the back of the sanctuary and told the One Church representative we were ready to get involved.

Along with others from our church who had been similarly compelled, we watched a brief video on foster care, and our formal training as foster parents started the following day. Despite being relative youngsters ourselves, God would use Tony's and my yes in wildly positive ways to come alongside young people who simply needed a shot at life.

The process for becoming foster parents was straightforward enough: after Tony and I completed our application, we were asked to commit to about thirty hours of home-study training that covered topics ranging from our legal rights as foster caregivers and what to expect regarding interaction with the children's biological parents to thoughtful child-development insights and cultural differences to be mindful of as we welcomed kids into our home and into our hearts. We were asked to submit all sorts of information—medical statements, financial records, and contact information for character references—and to complete a thorough background check. And finally, there was a series of home visits, where social workers checked and double-checked our place and our patterns to be sure that our lives would provide fertile soil in which a little boy or girl could grow. It was a Friday, late afternoon, when we'd received our final check marks, and to Tony's and my overjoyed astonishment, we were asked that same day to take in our first foster child.

. . .

"Gypsy Guy?" I asked the social worker, wanting to be sure I'd heard her correctly. "That's his given name?"

"You got it right," she said. "And his sister, who may be joining him later in your home, is Jayme Girl."

I stood there in our compact kitchen, grinning as I jotted down their names on a piece of scratch paper. "Got it," I said. "What time should we expect you two?"

Gypsy Guy was seven and was prone to telling stories. Or that's what I assumed, anyway, given that one of that sweet little boy's first autobiographical remarks to me referenced his "seven siblings who lived with nuns in California."

I knew he had a sister, but wouldn't the social worker have mentioned the other kids when she was giving me the lowdown on this boy's life? I trod carefully with him from the beginning, wondering if he would prove to be more mischievous than Tony and I had suspected, but within days, I knew I'd adopted the wrong strategy. Sure, there was his head of charming dark curls. And his melt-you-in-place eyes. But deeper still, the child was smart. *Unbelievably* smart. And he was kind—that much was easy to tell.

One afternoon, during a routine check-in with the social worker, I broached the subject of Gypsy Guy's family. "Are there other siblings besides the one sister?" I asked, to which she said, "Oh! Yes, in fact, there are. Gypsy and Jayme have seven other siblings who are living for now at a children's shelter run by a

Catholic church in Southern California." I grinned again. The little guy had gotten it exactly right.

"Gypsy was sent back here to Pittsburgh to live with his mom, but she wasn't able to keep things together enough to hang on to him. Still, we're all hoping she can rise to the occasion of getting all of her kids back. It's going to take a while, but we believe she will get there."

The social worker went on to tell me that the ultimate goal was to have all nine siblings together under one roof, and reflexively my heart sank. Despite the head count in the Dungy household totaling a meager two at the time, there was no way Tony and I could sign up for such a commitment. We were in our twenties, freshly married, and still trying to figure out who we were now that we were "one." I was teaching school full time. Tony had just started his NFL coaching career. We wondered if adding nine children to the mix would derail us in some sort of permanent way. "There may be a time when this could be a workable situation," I said to Tony, "but that time isn't now."

For more than a year, my darling Gypsy Guy would come in and out of our lives and our home with little to no warning. The poor boy would be shuttled here and there and everywhere while the adults responsible for him tried to sort out a solution, but more times than not, they were best-laid plans and nothing more.

On at least half a dozen occasions, Gypsy's mom would be scheduled for a custody hearing and not show. The morning of the hearing, Gypsy would look at me and say, "My mama's not coming. She never comes."

I would do my best to reassure him, despite my fears that his intuition was right. Sure enough, each evening of those scheduled hearings, the social worker would pull up to our house, Tony's little bachelor pad I'd freshened up for married life, and upon hearing our doorbell ring, I'd find a small face smooshed against our front glass. Gypsy Guy was ours once more. "What's for dinner, Mom Lauren?" he'd holler as he steamrolled us to get to the kitchen. "I'm *starving*."

The day came when we had to say goodbye to Gypsy Guy and his sister forever. Their caseworker was resolved to keep all the siblings together, and while I couldn't argue with the logic of that move, I thought my heart might shatter into a million pieces and I would completely lose it when I drew in that bundle of joy for a final hug. It was true: Tony and I couldn't hold on to those kids forever. But we could hold fast to our motivation for helping as many kids as we could. That motivation fuels us still today.

. . .

One of Pastor Farmer's favorite passages of Scripture to teach during his years at Bethany was the section in Matthew 25 that talks about the final judgment (verses 31-46). It's a passage distinctive in its ability to set our gaze on heaven while calling us to wise living here on earth, and each time Pastor read from it, something in me came alive. It's quite possible you've come across these verses before, but let me give them to you here again:

> But when the Son of Man comes in his glory, and
> all the angels with him, then he will sit upon his
> glorious throne. All the nations will be gathered
> in his presence, and he will separate the people as
> a shepherd separates the sheep from the goats. He

will place the sheep at his right hand and the goats at his left.

Then the King will say to those on his right, "Come, you who are blessed by my Father, inherit the Kingdom prepared for you from the creation of the world. For I was hungry, and you fed me. I was thirsty, and you gave me a drink. I was a stranger, and you invited me into your home. I was naked, and you gave me clothing. I was sick, and you cared for me. I was in prison, and you visited me."

Then these righteous ones will reply, "Lord, when did we ever see you hungry and feed you? Or thirsty and give you something to drink? Or a stranger and show you hospitality? Or naked and give you clothing? When did we ever see you sick or in prison and visit you?"

And the King will say, "I tell you the truth, when you did it to one of the least of these my brothers and sisters, you were doing it to me!"

Then the King will turn to those on the left and say, "Away with you, you cursed ones, into the eternal fire prepared for the devil and his demons. For I was hungry, and you didn't feed me. I was thirsty, and you didn't give me a drink. I was a stranger, and you didn't invite me into your home. I was naked, and you didn't give me clothing. I was sick and in prison, and you didn't visit me."

Then they will reply, "Lord, when did we ever see you hungry or thirsty or a stranger or naked or sick or in prison, and not help you?"

And he will answer, "I tell you the truth, when
you refused to help the least of these my brothers
and sisters, you were refusing to help me."
    And they will go away into eternal punishment,
but the righteous will go into eternal life.

    The first time I read those verses after meeting Gypsy Guy,
our ministry as foster parents felt to me like the most striking
example of these simple acts of service Jesus had lauded in his
followers. Gypsy had been a stranger. He'd come to us with
only the clothes on his back. He'd been thirsty and hungry . . .
goodness, the boy was *always* hungry. He'd needed hospitality
and care. He truly was one of "the least of these," and Tony
and I, despite all the things we lacked in terms of maturity and
know-how back then, had taken him in.

    If this was what following Jesus was to look like, was to *be*
like, then my husband and I were all in. We didn't have much,
but what we had, we'd share.

    We'd share it with kids in need of help.

    We'd share it with the least of these.

· · ·

You and I could debate who is the least of these and come
up with scores of answers. Even by Jesus' definition, "the least
of these" seems to include *anyone* who is down on their luck.
But the point is this: for those who are chronically hungry or
chronically thirsty or chronically unsheltered or chronically
unclothed or chronically lonely or chronically incarcerated—
whether fairly or unfairly—Jesus says, "Go there. Help them."

    Don't ask too many questions.

Don't think or pray too hard.

Just go.

Don't delay.

Go serve.

Go serve those in need *right now*.

I wonder if specific names or faces or groups of people are coming to mind for you as you read this. You might have family members who struggle to make it through each day in one piece. You might have a neighbor whose home life is marked by one tragic decision after another. You might know of people in your city who never have what they need to thrive. Who are "the least of these" that you tend to see? What simple gestures or resources would inject a little hope into their days?

For Tony and me, our answer to that "least of these" question has always centered on children. It seems to us that the stakes are much higher when children are the ones in need. Many adults have the life experience, the customary resourcefulness, and the time-earned stamina to survive hardship, even for an extended time. But place a child in the same set of tough circumstances, and their minds, hearts, and bodies will wither in a fraction of the time. They simply don't have the skill set to deal with suffering. They may be resilient, sure. But superhuman they are not.

This is, in part, why my husband and I had been drawn from the start to helping bring kids along in their respective journeys—Tony by coaching, me by teaching sixth-grade English, both of us by participating with Big Brothers Big Sisters of America, serving children in need overseas, and leading Sunday school classes in our church's children's ministry for years. So much *potential* resided inside each of those hearts, each of those minds. All they needed was a fighting chance.

We've always recognized that when you take in a child—for a brief hug or for months and months in your home—you help rewrite the code he or she is living by. In 2017, author Jason Reynolds wrote a bestseller titled *Long Way Down*. It was initially so well received that it was long-listed for the National Book Award for Young People's Literature, and once it hit the market, further awards kept rolling in. This book is about the code that urban youth live by. In the story, a boy named Will is determined to exact revenge on the person who killed his older brother, Shawn. In fact, Will heads upstairs to his family's eighth-floor apartment, retrieves the loaded gun his brother always hid in their shared bedroom, and begins the elevator ride back to the street, where he will hunt down the murderer and let retaliation have its way.

Why is this the plan? Because, according to his training, there is a three-part code you live by if you hope to survive life on the streets: part one, no crying; part two, no snitching; part three, always seek revenge. In other words, despite your suffering, hide the tears. Even if a police officer wants to help you, keep the facts to yourself. And regardless of competing morals, it's up to you to make things right.

The entirety of Reynolds's book takes place on that eight-floor elevator ride. It's a story that was evidently inspired by his own life. Reynolds had a friend get murdered on the streets and was determined to seek revenge. Would he go through with it? Would his character Will go through with it? How strong would that code prove to be?

I bring this up because it strikes at the core of why Tony and I do what we do. When children enter our presence—even if temporarily—they see order normalized. They see peace normalized. They see excellence normalized. They see a husband and wife treat one another with respect and work together to solve problems and communicate in a loving manner—both with each other and with the kids in the home. For a moment, the madness they're used to is cast aside. Nobody is yelling. Nobody is cussing. Nobody is drunk or high on drugs. There are no punches thrown, no slaps sustained, no doors kicked in, no mayhem allowed to unfold. In other words, they see what's *possible* when a different sort of code is upheld.

Today, according to groups who study these things, approximately 350 million children worldwide are living in extreme poverty, which is defined as existing on less than $1.90 per day. These boys and girls don't receive adequate nutrition. They don't receive adequate education. They don't receive adequate medical attention. They don't enjoy safety, or shelter, or peace.

In Hillsborough County, the general Tampa area of about 1.5 million people where Tony and I have lived for 25 years, at this writing, more than 2,000 kids live in out-of-home care. Of those children, just over 1,000 have been placed with a relative, about 800 have been placed in licensed foster care, between 200 and 300 live with a nonrelative of some sort, and about 225 live in group homes. The needs in each of these lives are all too real.

Not long ago, after Tony and I spent an afternoon reading our newest children's book to a school library full of second graders, the principal approached us to thank us for coming and said, "Bringing each of these kids a copy of your book was a very kind thing to do. These children don't have much, you know. A book to call their own is no small thing. . . ."

To help us understand just how under-resourced these students were, the principal went on to tell us that recently he and the teachers had needed to institute a "Friday-afternoon sweep" of the school each week, whereby the entire staff would scour every room in the school, looking for children who'd tucked themselves inside closets, underneath tables and desks, behind wall partitions, and beneath the bleachers in the gym.

Seeing that Tony and I weren't following the plot here, he said, "It's because this school is where 99 percent of them get their meals each day. They eat breakfast here. They eat lunch here. They get a snack here. So, on Fridays, they hide themselves away, believing that if they can be in this place on Saturdays and Sundays, they'll get food then, too."

These children weren't being fed anything nutritious at home. They would show up Monday morning utterly ravenous after two long days without food.

My heart leaped into my throat as I heard the principal explain the situation his young students faced. No child should ever go hungry in a world where abundance exists.

"But I've got to hand it to my teachers," the principal was saying. "While we can't allow students to spend weekends here, once our faculty realized the depth of the need, they banded together, pooled their dollars and cents, and started buying food for the kids to take home with them on Friday afternoons."

Roughly 350 million children worldwide are in situations just like this one, or worse. Here in my county, 2,000 boys and girls are in this predicament—a figure that is likely similar for yours.

Both of those are *really* big numbers—so big, in fact, that if we're not careful, we'll glaze right over them and assume there is nothing we can do to help. Which, in my view, would be a terrible misjudgment. Those statistics diminish as we come alongside one child at a time.

"Is it snack time?" Dontae said just yesterday with his infectious smile as he bounded into the room after preschool. He wrapped his arms around my midsection and buried his head in my lap.

"You're hungry again!" I said, laughing. Of *course* he was hungry again. "What are we in the mood for today?"

"Graham crackers!" he cheered, his little fist rising into the air, his chest puffing out his tiny Superman tee.

"Graham crackers it is," I said, rising to head for the kitchen, a miniature superhero nipping at my heels.

Maybe I couldn't fix the struggles his family was facing. But in those moments, as I helped get him settled in our safe home, amid the chatter and giggles of loving siblings, a plate of yummy food in front of him, I rubbed his back for a minute, thinking, *I pray this memory will matter, dear Dontae. I pray it will help you envision the life you deserve. . . .*

• • •

It's not lost on me that Tony and I never really expected to have a house full of kids. Or not *this* full, anyway. We had three children—Tiara, Jamie, and Eric—and as far as I could tell, Tony thought we were done. Three kids. Five members of the Dungy household in total. Five was a nice, round number, right?

I wasn't so sure.

When our youngest was eight, a member of Tony's coaching staff who happened to be a single man decided to adopt a son. He needed Tony's help to craft a work schedule that would allow for this major shift in his lifestyle, and he needed my help—and help from many other coaches' wives—to outfit his home and the nursery of the baby who would soon be his. The experience of helping him prepare for this new arrival was preparatory for me, too. "Tony," I said not infrequently during that season, "I think you and I should consider adopting a child."

Tony was forty-five years old at the time and worried that, given his age and the incessant demands on his time, it wasn't the right move. From a practical perspective, he had a point. But I truly believed I'd received a prompting from God to pursue adoption, and so Tony, to his credit, was all ears. I lost track of how many conversations we had across those weeks regarding how our little nuclear family would be affected by the addition of another child—an infant, no less. I leveraged every spare moment by providing Tony one more bit of information, one more piece of research, one more spiritual insight I'd gleaned. Over time, we both were led to the same conclusion: given the importance of every child to the heart of God, the practical needs that children right in our own zip code possessed, and our undeniable ability to pitch in and help, it was absolutely the right time for us to adopt. We brought home baby Jordan in August 2000, just six months after our first conversation with Heart of Adoptions, the agency that was helping us. Since then we have walked through this same process seven more times.

So far.

. . .

We've caught a lot of heat over the last many years from friends and acquaintances alike who look at Tony and me and ask,

"Why aren't you two just *enjoying yourselves* at this stage of life—traveling, taking up hobbies, relaxing a little, you know?"

You know what "stage of life" they mean, right? The one that says we're *old*. And given that Tony has hit the age when most people in this country officially retire and I'm not far behind him, I suppose that we aren't exactly spring chickens anymore. But I figure that if there is one way to stay young, it is by surrounding ourselves with youth. And, boy, do we have plenty of that around. Perhaps this was my own parents' life strategy, seeing as they fostered children well into their seventies. My grandmother Jessie Johnson had laid that course a generation earlier. She lost her husband from her first marriage to rheumatic fever when he was only thirty-two years old, but despite her terrible grief, she *still* took in children who weren't her own. She remarried, and she and her husband established their home as a rooming house, as it was called back then, for anyone who needed a place to stay for a day, a week, a month. My grandmother would cook for those people and love on them until they could get back on their feet, find decent work, and move on. She lived to be ninety-six years old and took in down-on-their-luck adults and plentiful foster kids well into her eighties.

By way of response to those friends and acquaintances, I always throw a question right back: "What on earth could be more enjoyable than what we're doing now?"

Listen, I know that some people dream of being my age because they think that *then* they will be able to travel the world or buy their dream house or lease the swanky new car. They think they'll finally be able to golf five days a week or read on the beach for hours without being interrupted or build that designer wardrobe they've always hoped to have. (To that last one, I should tell you that my sweet daughter Jade decided this past Mother's Day to make all the other kids and Tony pitch in to buy me a designer handbag, and while I was incredibly moved by the gesture, I had to ask Jade for coaching on how to wear it, and with what. Unless we're talking about running shoes, my attire intelligence is blissfully low.) They think that simply *accessorizing* their life will magically make it more fulfilling, despite their soul knowing full well that it won't.

What will satisfy?

What enjoyment will actually last?

• • •

I've always treasured time spent reading the Gospel accounts in Scripture—Matthew, Mark, Luke, and John—because it's there that Jesus gets to speak for himself. We don't just read *about* him in those four books; we read words spoken *from* him—from his mind, his heart, his mouth. A favorite passage for Tony and me alike is found in Mark 8, when Jesus is predicting his death for his disciples. "Then Jesus began to tell them that the Son of Man must suffer many terrible things and be rejected by the elders, the leading priests, and the teachers of religious law. He would be killed, but three days later he would rise from the dead," verse 31 says. "As he talked about this openly with his disciples, Peter took him aside and began to reprimand him for saying such things" (v. 32).

Jesus turned to his disciples, rebuked Peter for his lack of perspective, and told the onlookers who had surrounded him to hear his teaching: "If any of you wants to be my follower, you must give up your own way, take up your cross, and follow me. If you try to hang on to your life, you will lose it. But if you give up your life for my sake and for the sake of the Good News, you will save it" (vv. 34-35).

Then Jesus delivered this powerful pair of questions: "What do you benefit if you gain the whole world but lose your own soul? Is anything worth more than your soul?" (vv. 36-37).

He didn't wait for answers to those questions that day, instead concluding his message with a sobering reminder to them—and also to us. "If anyone is ashamed of me and my message in these adulterous and sinful days," he said, "the Son of Man will be ashamed of that person when he returns in the glory of his Father with the holy angels" (v. 38).

I think of the fleeting enjoyment of the best this broken world can offer, and I reflexively shake my head. *Uh-uh. Not for me. Not with so much on the line.*

Everyone else can have the dream house, the dream car, the string of dream vacations. You know what my dream is? It's Oprah calling me up one day and inviting me to her house for a lovely interview about the importance of caring for kids, only to blow my mind partway through our little chat by having all fifty or sixty of the children we've fostered along the way pop out and yell, "Surprise!"

I would laugh so hard at the sight of those precious faces that I'd dissolve into a puddle of tears. So many decades. So many memories. So much love.

I'd gather them up one by one into the tightest bear hug I could muster. I would look into each set of eyes: *Are you happy? Are you healthy? Are you whole?* I would introduce them, one to another. And then I'd praise my God in heaven above.

"Look at this life you've given me!" I'd tell him. "Look at this life you've given *us*."

Tony and I would come down from that emotional and spiritual high exactly never. Never! Can you imagine that glorious scene?

And you want to tell me there's something more *enjoyable* than filling out that crowd still more?

I dare you to even try. If there is one thing I know for sure in life, it is that the only way to know fulfillment is to totally give that life away.

And so, this book.

• • •

When Tony and I sat down to begin outlining the book you now hold in your hands, we had one main mission: we wanted to go back and revisit the handful of ways that God had prompted us to "give up our lives" for his sake along the way. What were the choices he'd asked us to make, and how had those various decisions led us to where we are today?

Those choices form the backbone for the chapters you're about to read, and while our yeses obviously have centered on serving children in need, once we jotted them down, we realized that they could apply to any sphere of service imaginable. In other words, our mission isn't pushing you to get trained for foster-care parenting and set your gaze on adopting kids who need forever homes. Rather, we hope that by sitting with the intentional choices we've made, and perhaps making a few of them in your own life, you will be better positioned to fulfill the specific service role that God has in store for *you*. And that the journey will be a great one for you.

1

BIG GOD

Choose to See Divinity

Tony

"What's the best advice you've ever been given?" Media outlets often have fun with this question, compiling answers from people of all walks of life, and the results are pretty inspiring to read. A few that have stood out to me along the way:

"Whatever you do, give it your all."

"The way someone treats you says more about them than about you."

"Your word is your bond."

"Nothing in life is free."

"Listen more than you speak."

"Don't harbor resentment. Holding on to bitterness is like drinking poison and expecting the other person to die."

For me, topping the list of the best advice I've ever received has to be a bit of wisdom from Chuck Noll, the first coach I played for in the NFL. I had just arrived in Pittsburgh, green as summertime grass, and was overjoyed to finally be able to chase my dream. I'd played football all my life but only had my sights set on going pro for a couple of years. At last, I'd made it. I'd arrived. I was actually going to be *paid* to play ball—that is, if I could secure a spot on the team. Millions of kids grow up wanting to gain entry onto the fields I'd be playing on, and the fact that I could become part of the tiny percentage of people who actually made it there caused my head to swim. I couldn't wait for Coach Noll to divulge the secret to making the cut.

You can imagine how disillusioning it was for me, then, when Coach gathered all us guys, sat us down, quieted us with his serious gaze, and said, "Gentlemen, welcome to the NFL. It's true: for many of you, playing football is about to be your official profession, but don't ever let it take over your life. Football is a profession. It is not a purpose. Big difference between the two. Do *not* make football your whole life. It is not your purpose. You have to find your purpose somewhere else."

I reflexively shook my head. *Huh?* We'd all finally gotten to the pinnacle, to a real NFL field, and now we were supposed to somehow downplay that accomplishment? I was dumbfounded. Coach's input broadsided me that day, but I tucked his words away. Years later, they'd come to mind again, and by then, I'd know what they meant.

. . .

I've had the opportunity to meet and talk with thousands and thousands of people over the years—just the nature of the work I've done. And almost without exception, whenever I've broached the subject of someone's purpose in life, they look at me like I've sprouted an extra eye. It's easy for people to tell me their profession—it's usually the first thing we ask someone, in fact. We find out their name and then instinctively say, "So what do you do?"

"I work in accounting," they say in response.

Or "I'm an optometrist."

Or "I work for the city."

Or "I'm still in school."

But while these answers can give us insight into how people spend their waking hours, they tell me nothing about the core of who they are. They reveal nothing about someone's *purpose* in life. Think of it this way: your profession is what you do, while your purpose is why you do it. Coach Noll's point to us first-year guys that day was that while it was fine to be professional football players, unless we had a driving motivation that went beyond racking up accolades and wins, we'd end up with a lackluster existence. We'd give everything to what was essentially a three- to five-year detour in life and be left empty-handed in the end.

When thinking about something as lofty as our life's purpose, I find it helpful to break it down a little right from the start. There are basically two ways of looking at purpose; keep reading to see which one better reflects your view.

In one camp, we have those who would say the world is theirs for the making. All that exists around them is raw material; how they form that raw material into the thing we call "life" is up to them. They are in charge of making meaning of the material; in other words, they are responsible for coming up with their purpose on their own.

In the other camp, we have those who would say, "No, there's a better way than that." They believe that the world already has a given order and a given meaning, and that their only role in this whole deal is discovering that order and meaning and shaping their lives in conformity to it.

You can probably guess that the second camp is where Lauren and I like to hang out. Both of us were raised by parents—grandparents, too, for that matter—who staked their claim on the idea that Creator God established everything in the natural world (including us humans) and purposed it from the start. The Genesis account of how the earth and everything in it came to be was sacred text to our parents because it bore out this belief that people are *special.* "So God created human beings in his own image," Genesis 1:27 confirms. "In the image of God he created them; male and female he created them."

All people are handcrafted in the image of God—*imago Dei*—and as such, they are set apart from the rest of creation. They are distinctive. They are God's crown. Because of this, passages like the apostle Paul's reminder to the church at Ephesus in Ephesians 1:3-8 were turned over like gems in the homes of our youth, carefully scrutinized, highly valued, tightly held. Those verses say,

> All praise to God, the Father of our Lord Jesus
> Christ, who has blessed us with every spiritual
> blessing in the heavenly realms because we are
> united with Christ. Even before he made the world,
> God loved us and chose us in Christ to be holy and
> without fault in his eyes. God decided in advance
> to adopt us into his own family by bringing us to
> himself through Jesus Christ. This is what he wanted
> to do, and it gave him great pleasure. So we praise

God for the glorious grace he has poured out on us
who belong to his dear Son. He is so rich in kindness
and grace that he purchased our freedom with
the blood of his Son and forgave our sins. He has
showered his kindness on us, along with all wisdom
and understanding.

There is a God, that passage confirms, and he knows us by
name. Before he set the intricacies of the world in motion, he
moved intentionally toward us. He loved us. He chose us. He
forgave us. And there's this part, which I love: he *decided in
advance* to welcome us into his family (v. 5) by making a way
for our sinfulness to be made right.

Lauren mentioned in the book's introduction that over the
years she and I have established various parameters for our lives
that make day-to-day operations a little easier in the Dungy
household, and if I had to cite the one reason why things are
running pretty smoothly for us still today, it's that we have pre-
decided the important stuff of life. I think it reflects the heart of
our heavenly Father when we decide some things "in advance,"
just as God did in adopting us as his daughters and sons. In
the same way that God decided in advance to pursue communion with us, the first pre-decision that Lauren and I made as
a couple was to pursue communion with him. The first of our
choices? It's to see God at work at every turn.

. . .

I've always loved the Old Testament character of Joshua, who
served as Moses' right hand before taking over leadership of
the nation of Israel himself. We know from that passing of the

baton that Joshua must have been daunted by his new responsibilities, which would include getting the Israelites across the
Jordan River and into the famed Promised Land. "No one will
be able to stand against you as long as you live," God promised
Joshua as he got going on this new mission. "For I will be with
you as I was with Moses. I will not fail you or abandon you"
(Joshua 1:5).

Even so, Joshua was unnerved. He'd spent so much time
working for Moses—which, by definition, meant working
toward the mission of reaching the Promised Land—that to
think about entering that place without his mentor must have
seemed all wrong. Not to mention undoable. In quick succes-
sion, God told Joshua to trust his—God's—presence and power
instead of his own. "Be strong and courageous," God said in
Joshua 1:6. "Be strong and very courageous," he repeated one
verse later. "Be careful to obey all the instructions Moses gave
you. Do not deviate from them, turning either to the right or to
the left. Then you will be successful in everything you do" (v. 7).

God reminded Joshua to study his Scriptures, meditating
on them "day and night" so the young leader would be careful
to do everything in them and so he could be prosperous and
successful (v. 8). Then, in verse 9, God reminded Joshua that
he wasn't alone in life, saying, "The LORD your God is with you
wherever you go."

It was God who was at work among his people.

All Joshua had to do was follow God's plan.

This is a clear picture of the kind of life Lauren and I want
to live—a life of uncommon influence. Like Joshua, we want to
be people who bring our weaknesses to God so his strength can
shine brighter still. We want to hear clearly from our Father. We

want to put our trust squarely in him. We want to help others take steps along God's path of righteousness. And then, upon achieving whatever it is that God has asked us to achieve, we want to push pause on all that laudable activity and thank the One who made everything work.

Another way of saying it: we want our life purpose to center on knowing God well so that we can also help make God known.

. . .

Despite the Pittsburgh Steelers' ruthless on-field reputation when I joined them in 1977—this was back in the day when their defensive line, led to four Super Bowl victories in six years by Mean Joe Green, was known as the Steel Curtain—it was there on that team that I found God. I'd "given my life" to the Lord years prior, when I was nine or ten years old. But in terms of truly surrendering my day-to-day world to his authority and authorship, I realized I hadn't trusted God with much of anything until a few fully devoted Steelers showed me how.

I noticed something special about those guys right from the start. Their demeanor was different, their words were life giving, and their energy level was off the charts every single day. They were real role models for me of faithfulness, righteousness, and joy. As I hung around them, I started becoming more like them. They taught me to prioritize daily Bible reading, extended times of private prayer, and weekly Bible studies. But more than anything else, they showed me how to serve others—not by what they said to me but by what they did. Over the twenty-four months that I played for Pittsburgh, those players taught me that it wasn't enough to say I believed in God or that I was a Christian. I needed to back those words up with actions—consistently, enthusiastically, sacrificially. They helped me see that if I went ahead and put these spiritual stakes in the ground, life would work better for me. As a result of putting God in first place in my life, my self-concept would be sharpened, my compassion for other people's struggles would deepen, and my desire to join God in his work to right the wrongs in the world would expand.

Fortunately, I followed them, and once I headed down that path, I never once looked back. By the time I met Lauren, I was deeply rooted in this lifestyle, and given that her passion for this way of life had been growing for years, as a couple we immediately bore fruit. It's fruit you can bear as well: you can learn to see yourself as God sees you. You can learn to see others as God sees them. And you can learn to spot serving opportunities that God longs for you to seize. These are the spiritual stakes I'm going to ask you to plant today. Not only will they make life work better for you, but they will help you influence those you come across for the better too.

SEE YOURSELF AS GOD SEES YOU

During that magical 2006 season in Indianapolis that resulted in a Super Bowl victory for our team, our guys hit a real rough patch. We'd had a 9–0 start to the season, which was fantastic, but then came a couple of close losses where we didn't play our best. That was followed by a catastrophe, a 44 to 17 loss to Jacksonville in December that felt like a knockout punch. It wasn't just an everyday loss; that defeat dashed our hopes for getting the top seed and a first-round bye in the playoffs. In one game's time, we'd fallen from the number one seed to number three, and despite our noteworthy start to the season, some were saying that this was it for the Colts.

It was embarrassing.

It was demoralizing.

The team looked at me expectantly in the locker room after the Jacksonville game. Something big was surely about to go down.

But that's not at all what occurred.

"We're not making any sweeping changes," I remember telling the team. "We're not bringing in any new players. We're not altering any major assignments. Nobody will be riding through those doors on a white horse to rescue us. We're not tapping some savior here."

I told the guys that the only thing we'd be doing going forward that season was getting back in touch with who we truly were. Allowing nearly four hundred rushing yards? Manning completing only half of his fifty passes? Assignment errors, mental breakdowns, sloppy play? We were more connected than what we'd shown on the field. We were tougher than we'd played. We were far more disciplined than we'd looked. This wasn't who we were. I told them the solution was simple—but not easy: we had to get back to our identity. We had spent six years constructing a team based on executing fundamentals, working hard, and fighting for each other. At our core, that's who we were, and this was no time to abandon our plan. There was nothing earth-shattering in my message. I offered not a magic formula but a stubborn determination to follow the plan.

We spent the next half hour talking as a team about what we'd been working toward, about the various pieces that we'd put in place to help us reach our goals, and wouldn't you know it—six weeks later, we were hoisting the Vince Lombardi Trophy, leaving many football "experts" shaking their heads over the wonder of it all.

It is no exaggeration to say that when we whisper this first yes in life—yes to God's existence, yes to God's sovereignty, yes to God's ongoing activity in and through our lives—we can rest assured that we will always, always win. Granted, it won't always *feel* like we're winning. There will be trials. There will be tribulations. There will be setbacks. There will be struggles that all but take our breath away. But we will live to tell about these wrestling matches. These losses won't take us out, as long as we follow the plan—God's plan.

· · ·

The apostle Paul, writing to believers in Corinth who were having trouble keeping their faith in God alive, reminded them that God "made this light shine in our hearts so we could know the glory of God that is seen in the face of Jesus Christ. We now have this light shining in our hearts, but we ourselves are like fragile clay jars containing this great treasure. This makes it clear that our great power is from God, not from ourselves" (2 Corinthians 4:6-7).

Then Paul continued: "We are pressed on every side by troubles, but we are not crushed. We are perplexed, but not driven to despair. We are hunted down, but never abandoned by God. We get knocked down, but we are not destroyed" (vv. 8-9).

I can't tell you how many times Lauren and I have felt knocked down by life, several of which we'll talk about in the pages to come. To know that such experiences simply *cannot destroy* the people who have tucked themselves under God's mighty wing has been a great comfort to us, and I suspect you'll find that truth comforting too. Just as Joshua was heartened by God's reminder that he is always with us, defending us, fighting our battles for us, seeing to it that we make it through whatever trials we face, Lauren and I garner great strength from knowing that God is on our side.

In the face of crushing burdens, we can be strong.

In the face of fearsome circumstances, we can be courageous.

When we stay tethered to our real identity, we can, as Paul promised in Philippians 4:13, "do everything" by the power of "Christ, who gives [us] strength."

So what is that *real identity*? Throughout Scripture, it's described in a variety of ways. Here are a few that have been most helpful to me over the years:

- We are accepted by Christ for the glory of God (see Romans 15:7).
- Those of us who have believed and accepted Jesus have been given the right to become God's children (see John 1:12).
- Once we are in Christ, "we are no longer slaves to sin" (see Romans 6:6).
- We are made complete by our "union with Christ, who is the head over every ruler and authority" (see Colossians 2:10).

In Christ, we are accepted. In Christ, we are embraced as daughters and sons of God. In Christ, we are freed from destructive patterns. In Christ, we are made totally and utterly *complete*. Regardless of who you are, where you've been, what you've done, and how you feel about all those things, this is very good news. No longer do we have to strive for acceptance. No longer do we have to hustle for approval. No longer do we have to writhe in the self-defeat that always accompanies chronic sin. No longer do we have to live fractured and fragmented lives. When we say yes to God—his existence, his eminence, his expert care for our lives—we say yes to a form of ourselves we've never seen before. This new model—this divinely transformed version of ourselves—is empowered by the Creator of the universe and, as such, can do things we simply cannot do on our own.

. . .

As I made my way through my adolescent years, I was so driven by the competitive nature of sports—basketball, primarily, but also football and track—that I got myself in trouble now and then. I was this way in school, too, I guess, always pushing for the A, thinking that my GPA or being accepted into a certain college would show everyone that I was smart. But anyway, in athletics, I'm not proud to say that this drive to succeed made me a pretty insufferable guy. I hated to lose, because I wanted to prove to everyone that I was the best athlete they had ever seen. And worse than that, I was a know-it-all. I had the answer to every problem my team faced, and I wasn't afraid to let them know what it was. I even up and quit the football team one year because I was offended by something my coach had said. You get the idea.

I was a hothead.

A sore loser.

A sore winner as well, truth be told.

Those traits followed me through high school and college, but more times than not, my boorish behavior was written off as the "competitive" nature of a talented player. In my case, it was not so much competitiveness as it was immaturity. I needed to grow up some.

Interestingly, once I got a few years of maturity on me, graduated from high school, allowed college to smooth some of my rough edges, and met those Steelers my rookie year in the NFL, things began to shift. The truth of my identity began to sink in: that I was accepted and approved, that I was no longer a slave to sin. I began to understand that because I was "in Christ," I was whole and holy and healthy and secure. I didn't have to prove anything to anyone. I had all that I needed in God, and I could start living like that was true. I was still ultracompetitive. I just had a new approach to competing now.

In the same way that drawing a fussy baby into your chest allows your calm, steady heartbeat to lower the heart rate of that upset child, each time I chose to draw strength from God's reservoir instead of mustering power of my own, all that amperage I'd been carrying around would settle down in me. The wildfire blazing through my nostrils, my mind, my veins, would supernaturally start to burn out. I still had the drive to win—make no mistake about that. But now I realized I could win without leaving a path of destruction in my wake.

I wonder if you can relate.

Maybe you, too, have seen some tendencies in your attitude or actions that are a little . . . out of control. Maybe your "passion" has started spilling over into rage-fueled outbursts toward the people you care about most. Perhaps the desire for excellence at work has morphed into a standard of perfection that neither you nor your colleagues can meet. It could be that your appreciation for thoroughness is now an outright control issue that those in your sphere of influence are finding tough to take. I don't know what it is for you, but my guess is that you do. And you probably realize that if that pattern of behavior is left unchecked, it will surely take you down.

Is it argumentativeness?

Is it defensiveness?

Do you always need the spotlight on you?

Do you have to be the best?

Do you have to win the debate?

Do you need others' blessing to feel good about yourself?

The need to earn acceptance and approval, to prove our worth each day, can make us do some crazy things. Equally true: when we lay down all that hustling and humbly come before God, he infuses us with a level of confidence and peace that Scripture says simply can't be understood (see Philippians 4:7). This is key, because when you and I misjudge, misapprehend, misunderstand, or misbehave, our lives aren't the only ones we affect. There's always someone else on the receiving end of that mistake, wouldn't you agree? And based on (way too much) firsthand experience, we can't be helpful to someone we are simultaneously harming. We can't bash and bless someone at the same time.

SEE OTHERS AS GOD SEES THEM

My family's home is situated about a fifteen-minute drive from one of the greatest theme parks in the country, Tampa Bay's Busch Gardens. You'll recall that Lauren and I have a *lot* of kids and that we've had a lot of kids for nearly three decades now. Suffice it to say, we've been to Busch Gardens a few times. We went three weeks ago, in fact, to celebrate our daughter Jaela's sixth birthday, and despite giving her complete power over which rides the family rode, everyone had a fantastic time.

I'm no expert on the subject, but in my opinion, some of the best people watching happens at theme parks. You see everything there: wild fashion choices, curious parenting techniques, questionable food-fare decisions, the whole works. There have been times when I was waiting on one of our kids who had to run to the restroom, sitting idly on a bench with some members of our family while the other members rode a particular ride, or hanging out at an outdoor dining table while our kids finished lunch. With nothing to do for a few minutes, I'd just watch all the people walking by. It's entertaining, right? So many kids and adults from so many walks of life; so much diversity packed into one tourist attraction; so many preferences, capabilities, habits, and nuances represented there—just incredible to behold.

On one such occasion, I remember sitting there thinking, *I wonder what God is up to in their lives.*

It almost became a game to me that day. I'd see a guy staffing a roller coaster—ushering everyone onto the ride, checking that lap bars were secure, and pushing the button to make the ride go—and I'd whisper to God, *Are you working in that young man's heart?*

I'd see a mom with two kids in a stroller and an infant strapped to her chest, withered from the humidity and heat, and I'd think, *God, are you working in that woman's heart?*

I'd see the teenager tasked with refilling people's sodas and ask, *What's up with him, Father? Are you working on him at all?*

In two of the four Gospel accounts in Scripture, we learn that when Jesus saw a large group of people, he looked at them "with compassion." For instance, Matthew reports that "Jesus traveled through all the towns and villages of that area [the region of Capernaum], teaching in the synagogues and announcing the Good News about the Kingdom. And he healed every kind of disease and illness. When he saw the crowds, he had compassion on them because they were confused and helpless, like sheep without a shepherd" (Matthew 9:35-36).

As I read those verses, I see the importance of not just being *superficially entertained* by the people we see day in and day out but, rather, being *spiritually engaged* with them. Sure, it's natural to elbow your spouse and subtly nod toward the person across the way who is boasting a "look" that is unlike anything you'd ever voluntarily wear, but that reaction does nothing to signal to God that you're available to be of service to him.

Since I've known Lauren, she and I have worked diligently to stay motivated not by categorization but by compassion. Categorization is making assumptions based on people's outward appearance instead of letting God show you something of their heart. It's putting people in "buckets" before exchanging a single word with them: they're old; they're foolish; they're disrespectful; they're crude; they're impulsive; they're rebellious; they're haughty; they're dangerous; they're obnoxious; they're _____. We fill in that blank with all sorts of descriptors, even when we have never so much as *met* the person we've judged.

Guess how many buckets Jesus had? One. It was labeled *people he loved.*

Because he saw people as sheep in need of a shepherd, compassion was free to bubble up in his heart. Sheep that don't have a shepherd, incidentally, are in real danger of becoming lost, being stolen, or getting killed. Jesus was able to look beyond appearances and focus on the actual person inside because he *hated* those tragic outcomes for the people he'd come to serve.

He didn't want anyone to stay lost.

He didn't want anyone to be snatched from his grip.

He certainly didn't want anyone to die—not on his watch, anyway.

And so, moved by boundless compassion, he spiritually engaged with them.

. . .

A few years ago, I was inducted into the NFL Hall of Fame, and along with the others who were enshrined that evening, I was asked to give a speech. I labored over those words, not wanting to forget to thank any of the friends, family members, coaches, or colleagues who'd made it possible for me to enjoy three decades in the league as both player and coach. And while my words that night felt unique to my history, my experience, and my life, I couldn't help but notice that all the speeches at the ceremony shared a similar theme. The names were different, but every one of us spent a fair amount of time thanking the people who had seen something in us that nobody else seemed to see. The ones who took a shot on us when there was no good reason to do so. The ones who believed in us even when we didn't believe in ourselves.

I think back on my upbringing in the small automotive town of Jackson, Michigan, and remember with a smile the guys who thought I was special when I wasn't, who extended kindness to me when I didn't deserve it, who were generous with me to a fault despite having a thousand other ways they could have spent their money and time. Robert Burton, an older friend of mine, ran the rec center in Jackson, and when I was nine or ten years old, he'd say, "Tony, the gym closes at six, but if you and your buddies ever want to come and just shoot baskets or hang out, you call me, and I'll come open up. If you don't have a place to be, you can be here."

Frank Hampton was my barber for years, and I can recall scores of conversations we had while I was sitting in his chair, a towel draped around my neck. "Make me look good," I'd tell him. "Game tonight, you know . . ." Mr. Hampton not only cut my hair on those occasions, but he also tended to my soul. He'd ask questions about how my family was doing and whether we'd gone to church that week. He wanted to know what I'd been learning about God and whether my priorities were still ordered right.

Alan Truman was a friend of mine six years older than I. He made a habit of taking me under his wing. You'd think an eighteen-year-old would have better things to do than take a twelve-year-old kid to Friday night baseball games and football games or hang out for an hour tossing a ball in the park or go for walks so he could talk to me about how to get through my teenage years without succumbing to the drug culture that had infiltrated our neighborhood—so many neighborhoods, truth be told. But this was how Alan chose to spend his time, week after week, year after year. I didn't comprehend the depth of that investment until I was eighteen or nineteen myself, but once I saw it, I couldn't unsee it. Alan Truman had given me things

I'd never, ever be able to pay back: insight, wisdom, know-how, savvy, courage, and belief in myself.

I remain grateful to him to this day.

My point in all of this is that, without exception, the people I knew in my childhood who were most devoted to Jesus were the same folks who were most devoted to me. Because they loved God, they had the capacity to love me. And I wasn't always very lovable, if I'm shooting straight. I look back on those relationships now and understand that their acceptance and inclusion weren't riding on my performance but, rather, on the potential they saw in me.

In the Old Testament book of 1 Samuel, God asked the prophet Samuel to anoint a new king for the Israelite people after King Saul was rejected by God for disobeying a direct command from the Lord. He directed Samuel to Bethlehem, where Samuel would find a man named Jesse. God explained that the new king would come from that specific household of faith. As the prophet set out on his journey, God gave him this advice: "Don't judge by his appearance or height, for I have rejected him. The LORD doesn't see things the way you see them. People judge by outward appearance, but the LORD looks at the heart" (v. 16:7). Small detail, but God told Samuel this after he'd tried to select the first brother.

With that counsel in mind, Samuel reached Jesse and began interviewing his many sons. Abinadab—nope. Shimea—nope, not him either. "All seven of Jesse's sons were presented to Samuel," the text says, but "the LORD [had] not chosen any of these" (v. 10).

Samuel, confused by this point as to who on earth God had tapped for this all-important position, said, "Do you have any other sons you haven't told me about?" to which Jesse said, "There is still the youngest, . . . but he's out in the fields watching the sheep and goats" (v. 11). Translation: he's not the kid you're looking for. He's barely six feet tall. He's slight of build. He wouldn't know a tight spiral if it popped him in the face.

Yet that unimpressive youngest kid was *precisely* the one God had tapped. When David showed up, having come in from the fields where he was working as a glorified livestock babysitter, "the LORD said, 'This is the one; anoint him'" (v. 12).

Those mentors of mine believed that once I was living surrendered to God's ways instead of my own, the sky was the limit for me. The world may have judged me according to the externals—how I looked, how athletic I was (or wasn't), my personality, my temper, my grades. But God—and those who served him—saw only my heart . . . and what might become of that heart someday. And so, believing the best for me, and disregarding what they were observing firsthand, my parents, my extended family, and those men worked to point me in the right direction—toward God.

. . .

I think about those selfless contributions a lot as I go through my day-to-day life all these years later. I try to give others the same acceptance, affection, and belief that those mentors gave me. As I encounter other people, I try to remember that they are God's image bearers in a very broken world. I try not to focus on any external characteristics that might taint my perception of them—how they look, how they're dressed, how they're behaving, what they say. Instead, I try to picture them as they could be, perfectly surrendered to the Lord Jesus and exhibiting his attributes to the world.

None of us will ever get to that state of holy perfection in this life. But I find that when I focus on that ideal, it helps me treat others the way God himself has treated us all. In the apostle Paul's letter to the church at Rome, he told the Roman congregation how God regarded them:

> When we were utterly helpless, Christ came at just the right time and died for us sinners. Now, most people would not be willing to die for an upright person, though someone might perhaps be willing to die for a person who is especially good. But God showed his great love for us by sending Christ to die for us while we were still sinners. And since we have been made right in God's sight by the blood of Christ, he will certainly save us from God's condemnation.
>
> ROMANS 5:6-9

This same perspective can be ours when we say yes to God's activity in the world. We can approach *every person we meet* not in a spirit of condemnation but rather in a spirit of compassion, of grace. Recently, after Dontae and baby Kallie had been in our care for a few days, their caseworker let us know that the children's mom would be connecting with the kids by Skype the following afternoon and that we would need to facilitate that virtual meeting.

It came as no surprise to me that Lauren's reflexive reaction to that news was to pray. Rather than judge the woman who birthed these beautiful children for the life choices that led to their removal from her care, she sat there and prayed. Because she understands that all of us have sinned against God—herself included—she thanked him for the grace that covers every foible, failure, mistake, and misstep. She asked God about his plans for the kids' mom—"What are you up to in her life, Lord?" she prayed. "How can I encourage her? What questions should I ask? How are you working even now to redeem this whole situation and to reunify the kids and their mom?"

There's something a lot like Jesus going on in our hearts when we see others as God sees them.

Sixteen years ago, Lauren and I received unimaginably painful news. Our teenage son Jamie had died. Complicating this tragedy was the fact that his death was quickly ruled a suicide, a reality that would baffle us for years. Just like that, our warm, loving gentle giant was gone.

We believe what Romans 8:28 says, that "God causes everything to work together for the good of those who love God and are called according to his purpose for them." It would take some time, but eventually God would give us glimpses of the good he was working from that devastating tragedy. Amid the outpouring of support from people who'd known and loved Jamie—the emails, the letters, the voice-mail messages, the cards—came confirmation that our request for Jamie's organs to be donated had been received and processed and that waiting donor-recipients would soon be notified. Amazingly, we'd even been able to donate Jamie's corneas. I hadn't even known that was possible.

About a year after Jamie's death, we got word that two people had each received one of Jamie's corneas and now at last could see. I thought about all that Jamie had seen through those eyes—the people nobody else saw, the outcasts nobody else thought to include, the needs nobody else stopped to meet—and I wondered if those transplant recipients now saw the world that way too. To Jamie, people were never an intrusion or an inconvenience. They were an invitation to see, to know, to love, to care, to serve.

People were never a distraction. They were a divine appointment in the works.

People were never a burden. They were a *blessing* sent straight from God.

Who are you? How are you? What do you need? How can I help? These questions formed the ticker that ran incessantly at the bottom of Jamie Dungy's heart.

There's a story in Mark 8 about a blind man who begged Jesus to heal him. Jesus took the blind man by the hand, led him to a quiet place, and spat on the man's eyes, which I've always found an odd touch. He laid hands on the blind man and said, "Can you see anything now?" The man looked around and said, "Yes, I see people, but I can't see them very clearly."

Jesus put his hands on the man again and completely restored his vision. (See Mark 8:22-26 for the full story.)

Help those people who now have Jamie's eyes, I prayed to God, *to see as Jamie saw.*

The truth is we'd all be better off seeing as Jamie saw.

SEIZE OPPORTUNITIES TO SERVE

When we say yes to God—his presence, his power, his redemptive activity in the world—we start seeing ourselves as God himself sees us. We start seeing *others* as God sees them too. And then there's this: we start seizing opportunities for service that are ours alone to seize.

Throughout Scripture, we are reminded that faith without works is faith that is totally dead. This is crystal clear to us in the book of James, where we read these words:

> What good is it, dear brothers and sisters, if you say you have faith but don't show it by your actions? Can that kind of faith save anyone? Suppose you see a brother or sister who has no food or clothing, and you say, "Good-bye and have a good day; stay warm and eat well"—but then you don't give that person any food or clothing. What good does that do?
>
> So you see, faith by itself isn't enough. Unless it produces good deeds, it is dead and useless.
>
> JAMES 2:14-17

Here, we are reminded that it's never enough just to *see as God sees*; we're also meant to *serve as he would serve*. This can seem burdensome at first blush. Who has the time and energy to serve others when most of us have our hands full just keeping our own lives afloat? We will spend the entirety of chapter 5 answering that question, but for now let me say this: once you start to see yourself as God sees you, and you start to see others as God sees them, serving the needs you discover around you will be the most natural thing you can do.

In the Dungy household of my youth, my mom and dad, Cleomae and Wilbur, always told my siblings and me that impact was far more important than income. Sure, they taught us to work hard so we could have good jobs. But that work was never to be the focal point of our lives. It was *relationships* that were most important.

Hold the Lord in high regard.

Hold others in high regard.

Be prepared to share with others, as Jesus has shared with you.

These were formative beliefs for us Dungy kids.

May they be formative for you as well.

2

AGAINST THE GRAIN

Choose Integrity

Tony

Over the years, I've met people from all walks of life, and while their vocations differ, there seems to be something inside them that longs for excellence, that craves success in their given fields. Of course, I've seen this drive in scores of athletes and coaches who are always vying for the next win, the next record, the next championship. But I've also seen it in business executives who live chronically captivated by landing the next client, signing the next contract, netting the next deal. I've seen it in pastors who are forever trying to outpace last year's numbers—attendees, salvations, baptisms, conference participants, and more. I've seen it in actors and musicians desperate for the breakthrough role or big event. I've seen it in philanthropists who seem incapable of resting until their names are engraved for all to see on one building or another. I've seen it in new moms, even, who obsess over the latest parenting trends in hopes of "getting it right."

For most people, there is the sense that whatever we've chosen to do in life, we want to do it well. We want to excel. We want to be the best. If there is a commendation given, we want to have it. If there is an award bestowed, we want to receive it. If there is a record kept, we want to own it. Nobody wants to be known as below average in an endeavor he or she cares deeply about. Most people play to win, right?

We want to play to win.

We want to be known for greatness.

We want to be recognized for having done something really well.

To that last point, I'd have to admit that during the early days of my head-coaching career, it was pretty fun to be recognized whenever I was out and about in the world. I'd be out to dinner with my family in Tampa, and within minutes, everyone seemed to know that the Bucs coach was in the house. I have to admit that it does help your ego to have people approach you with compliments about your work and ask for your autograph or for you to pose for a selfie with them. But it can get old quickly. Sometimes you want to dart into a convenience store for a bottle of water without being stopped half a dozen times, you know?

Lauren got sick of the trend even before I did. One especially annoying situation that comes to mind was when Lauren and I were at a restaurant with a few of our kids. Lauren got up from the table to use the restroom and returned to find another woman sitting in *her* seat. The woman, a longtime Bucs fan, was leaning forward on her forearms, speaking in an animated fashion to my kids and me, and as she spoke, I noticed that little droplets of spit kept falling onto Lauren's plate of food, which had been delivered while Lauren was away. Once the fan extricated herself from our table, my wife, shaking her head and chuckling over the woman's audacity, asked our server to please replace her meal.

After I took the job with NBC doing the Sunday Night Football broadcast, my recognition throughout the country grew greater still. By that time, I tried to make some of the interruptions as brief as possible. "Has anyone ever told you that you look like Tony Dungy?" someone would say to me, to which I'd nod and with a grin say, "Yeah. I get that a lot."

You'd be surprised by how many people would just shake their heads over the coincidence and walk away.

Last summer, while on vacation with my family in Oregon, one guy came up to me at a skate park, where I was hanging out with my sons, and said, "You look really familiar."

I nodded, assuming I knew where this was headed, but then he said, "You work at Lowe's, don't you? I think you helped me with my faucets last week."

We want the success. We want the reward. We want the attaboys, the attagirls, from a fickle watching world. But once we get it, we realize it's not all it's cracked up to be. Actor and comedian Jim Carrey once wished that "everyone could get rich and famous and everything they ever dreamed of so they can see that's not the answer."[1]

I don't know if Mr. Carrey and I would agree on what *is* the answer, but I concur that it definitely is not fame.

THE ULTIMATE PRIZE

An interviewer asked me recently for my thoughts on the current class being inducted into the Pro Football Hall of Fame and then said, "That's *it*, right? In terms of an NFL career, there's no higher award than that."

She then asked, "I mean, what does it mean to *you* to know that you'll be honored forever in that way?"

I nodded and smiled. I got why she'd asked the question, and I knew what she thought I would say.

For people in my line of work, the Hall of Fame is the ultimate prize. Being enshrined is the capstone on a career that tells the watching world that while you may not have gotten everything right, you must have gotten *something* right. Which is probably why the answer I gave her wasn't exactly what she expected me to say.

"Not as much as you might think," I replied with a laugh.

Granted, getting the nod from the Hall of Fame is an extremely high honor. It was incredible to join the ranks of some of the all-time football greats, players and coaches alike: Art Rooney, Joe Greene, Jim Brown, Gale Sayers. It was deeply satisfying to know that a big reason I was being inducted was that I'd coached a team to a Super Bowl victory and that I'd been the first African American coach to do so. (That fact showed up as a *Jeopardy!* answer one time, which was kind of fun.) Actually, when Lovie Smith's Chicago Bears and my Indianapolis Colts faced off in Super Bowl XLI, it was the first time a Black coach had even made it to the Super Bowl. That day in 2007, two had done so. Innumerable opportunities have come my way—not the least of which is the analyst job I presently hold—as a result of being a "Hall of Famer." Whenever I consider those opportunities, I shake my head in disbelief. When I was thirteen, fourteen years old, all I wanted to do was play a game. I wanted to compete in a sport—any sport.

Actually, progress for me back then would have been beating my mom at anything athletic in nature. It wasn't that I was weak or unskilled; it was just that she possessed wild natural talent in every sport she picked up.

"Just let me in the game"—that was the earnest cry of my heart. To think that God allowed me not just into the game but also to reach the very pinnacle of a game I deeply love is astounding to me still today. So, then, why doesn't that prize of a Hall of Fame induction hold greater meaning for me than it does? Because it was never the ultimate goal.

When it's all said and done, enshrinement in the Pro Football Hall of Fame isn't the reward I most desire. I've got my eyes fixed on a far different prize.

WHAT GOD IS AFTER

If you're familiar with the Bible, you may have heard the parable about the three servants and the bags of gold. As the story goes—you can find the full account in Matthew 25:14-30—a man who is leaving for a long journey brings together his servants and entrusts his wealth to them, giving each of them a different amount based on their ability to manage money well. One servant receives five bags of gold, another two, and a third just a single bag, but while the bag count varies, one thing remains the same: the master expects every servant to increase his wealth while he is away.

Two are successful. One? Not so much.

The five-bagger gained another five: a 100 percent increase—pretty good.

The two-bagger gained two more: equally good.

"But the man who had received one bag," Matthew 25:18

says, "went off, dug a hole in the ground and hid his master's money" (NIV).

Not the guy's best day, right?

The master returns from his trip ready to settle his accounts, and you know the truth is going to come out. He finds the servant he'd left five bags with and learns he's doubled the master's sum. "Well done, good and faithful servant! You have been faithful with a few things; I will put you in charge of many things. Come and share your master's happiness!" (v. 21).

The same scene unfolds for the servant who'd gained two bags. *Well done! You've been faithful! Come, celebrate with me!*

But then comes the interaction between the master and the guy who'd been given one bag. "Master," the servant said, "I knew that you are a hard man, harvesting where you have not sown and gathering where you have not scattered seed. So I was afraid and went out and hid your gold in the ground. See, here is what belongs to you" (vv. 24-25).

The master was so enraged that he was shaking. "You wicked, lazy servant!" he boomed (v. 26). He ordered his men to throw the worthless servant outside into the darkness, "where there will be weeping and gnashing of teeth" (v. 30).

The "weeping and gnashing of teeth" part is what may have tipped you off that there is a deeper meaning to this story than just a master looking to grow his money. We are those servants. God is our master. And the stewardship expectation rests on us. God is looking for followers of his who won't just sit on the gifts and talents he's given us but who instead will invest those resources wisely, believing that God will use those investments for good.

He's looking for us to be faithful, in other words—to live each day by *faith*.

WALKING THE TALK

If you were asked to define *integrity*, which words would you use? The dictionary says integrity is "the quality of being honest and fair" and "the state of being complete or whole."[2] If you're a word nerd, you might know that *integrity* as we know it and spell it today originated in the fourteenth century with the Old French word *integrité*, which means "innocence" or "blamelessness." It's from the Latin root word *integer*, referring to a whole number, which is also a root for the word *integrate*, meaning assimilate, incorporate, or fully mix in.

In the context of your spiritual life, integrity is simply the practice of matching your walk to your talk. You do what you say and say what you do. Instead of just giving lip service to your beliefs, you live them out. Integrity is what's happening when Christ followers are actually following Christ. (Novel idea these days, isn't it?)

In chapter 1, we looked at the ideas that we have been made complete in Christ, that God is at work redeeming all that has been marred by sin in the world, and that you and I are invited every day to join God in his good work. These ideas are at the center of our purpose in life. And while lots and lots of people would look at me right now and nod their heads and say, "Yeah, yeah . . . I'm good with all of that," very few people are willing to *live* according to these beliefs. Based on our definition above, those very few people possess a key quality of the Christ-following life: integrity.

Integrity is *doing* what you believe.

· · ·

In the first century, monastic communities started popping up all throughout Italy, and one man was to thank. His name was St. Benedict, and he was absolutely fascinated with the idea of crafting a lifestyle of integrity. He wanted to sort out the rhythms and practices that would make for the ideal monk— and not only did he sort them out, but he also lived by them for decades. Those patterns became known as the Rule of St. Benedict, and across the centuries since his death, much has been written about how to apply "the Rule" in modern life.

If you were to whittle the entire Rule to its absolute core, you'd find one character trait sitting there: humility.

Humility. St. Benedict was taken with the sentiment found in Luke 14:11, which says, "For all those who exalt themselves will be humbled, and those who humble themselves will be exalted" (NIV). According to the famous monk, the central quality a Christ follower must possess is humility; all else stems from that initial willingness to surrender to the ways of God.

Benedict even crafted what he named the "ladder of humility," intending to show the twelve specific steps a person must take to engage deeper and deeper in humility's work. I bring this up because the first two steps of that ladder happen to coincide directly with the first two topics we have covered in this book: first, we acknowledge the presence and goodness of God, and second, we surrender our will to his. In Benedict's words, those two steps read this way:

1. The fear of God.

"The first degree of humility, then, is that a man always

have the fear of God before his eyes . . . and that he be ever mindful of all that God [has] commanded."

2. Not my will, but yours, O Lord.

"The second degree of humility is, when a man [loves] not his own will, nor is pleased to fulfill his own desires but by his deeds [carries] out that word of the Lord which [says]: 'I came not to do My own will but the will of Him that sent Me'".[3]

Monks the world over began living according to Benedict's Rule, which prioritized things like Bible reading and praying and spending quality time with God above things that most of us would say are important endeavors in life: eating, sleeping, hanging out with friends. The monks did these things because they took seriously the job of stewarding well the resources that God had entrusted to them—time and energy and real skills. They didn't want to have Jesus return on their watch and call them wicked, lazy servants. They wanted to hear a far different message from him, something that sounded like "Well done, good and faithful servants . . ."

I read of commitment like that, commitment that stands in such stark contrast to how so much of the world runs, and I am reminded that sometimes standing apart from the crowd is the wisest place to be.

• • •

The apostle Paul had something to say about this subject matter as well. In his letter to the believers in Rome, he wrote this:

Therefore, I urge you, brothers and sisters, in view of God's mercy, to offer your bodies as a living sacrifice, holy and pleasing to God—this is your true and proper worship. Do not conform to the pattern of this world, but be transformed by the renewing of your mind. Then you will be able to test and approve what God's will is—his good, pleasing and perfect will.

ROMANS 12:1-2, NIV

To understand what Paul was saying when he told believers not to conform to the pattern of the world, we just need to look around us and see what's popular in the culture in which we live. Sure, technology was different back in Paul's time, but the human heart was exactly the same. Impatient. Petty. Selfish. Sinful. Greedy. The list goes on. Paul, in short, was saying, "Don't be that way. Be the opposite of all that."

It may not be easy, but it is straightforward. If you and I will believe that God exists and has our best interests at heart, and if we will decide to loosen the grip on our own will and ways and tighten our grip on his, we will be doing exactly what Paul said to do. We will be followers of Jesus who are *actually following him.*

It's true that this kind of living feels like a sacrifice, which is the term Paul used in Romans 12:1. But I'm telling you from firsthand experience that once you decide to live by God's plan, you'll save yourself from lots of pain and grief. Think of it: you don't have to cover up a sin you never committed. You don't have to perpetuate a lie you never told. You don't have to hide a habit you never picked up. Righteousness may require sacrifice initially, but over time? Right living is a *relief.* I caught a vision for this idea back in Pittsburgh when I was a rookie beginning my NFL career and have held on to it ever since. The Hall of Fame is pretty cool—I'll admit it. But the real reward I'm after? It's more like a Hall of *Faith.*

HALL OF FAITH-ERS

To read chapter 11 of the book of Hebrews is to catch a glimpse of life lived well. The entire chapter is only forty verses long, but in that short space, we get a rundown of people who refused to go the way of the world, instead choosing to honor God with their lives. These folks weren't content with talking the talk; they also walked the walk. By faith, Abel brought a better offering to God than his brother did. Enoch was so faithful that he didn't have to experience death. Noah built the ark by faith. Abraham left his homeland by faith. Isaac and Jacob lived out that faith as well. Sarah was too old to have kids but trusted that she would—by faith. Joseph, Moses, Rahab, David, Samson, Samuel, and many others may not have gotten everything right in life, but when history told their stories, those stories were stitched together by *faith.* They were sure about what they believed, and those beliefs governed their lives—Hall of Faith-ers, each one.

I've been asked many times what I hope my legacy will be after my days on earth are done, and my answer is always the same. I want to be known as a man of integrity, a man who was faithful to God. Hall of Faith, here I hopefully come.

The thing is I'm not naturally these things. In my own power, in my own strength, and relying on my own creative initiative, I can't get the "faithful integrity" thing done. I need supernatural empowerment because these are supernatural goals. So, in the space that remains in this chapter, I want to lay out three reminders that help me stay this course, three truths that could land us *both* in the Hall of Faith. You ready? Here they are:

1. The call is constant.
2. The struggle is real.
3. It's never too late to get right with God.

THE CALL IS CONSTANT

Back when I was twenty-one years old, the most impactful spiritual truth that I picked up from those veteran Steelers was based on that passage from Romans 12. It went like this: if I was supposed to offer my body as a "living sacrifice" to the Lord, then that living sacrifice had to be offered *wherever my body was*.

This news was revolutionary to me.

See, it's easy to think that we can be one way, say, at church and another way on the football field. But what those guys taught me is that living two different ways is not the path of integrity. When I was at church, I needed to offer my body— mind, heart, soul, spirit—to God as a living sacrifice. When I was on the football field, I needed to offer myself to God as a living sacrifice there, too.

When I was in the locker room with my teammates, I needed to offer myself to God as a living sacrifice.

When I went home to Lauren, I needed to offer myself to God as a living sacrifice.

When I was in the meeting room taking notes, I needed to offer myself to God as a living sacrifice.

When I went to the grocery store and to restaurants and to the bank, I needed to offer myself to God as a living sacrifice.

When I was on the team plane headed to an away game, I needed to offer myself to God as a living sacrifice.

When I showed up for practice and was told to run wind sprints, I needed to offer myself to God as a living sacrifice.

I think you get the idea. At all times, *wherever my body was*, I needed to not just say that I believed in God. I also needed to surrender to him.

Still today, wherever my body goes, it is there that I need to offer myself as a living sacrifice to God.

And the same is true for you.

If you're a teacher, you can be a person of integrity not just when you're standing at the front of the room instructing but also when you're managing a challenging student or dealing with a biased principal or suppressing prejudice of some sort if it rises in your own heart as you're grading papers.

If you're a writer, you can be a person of integrity not just when you're typing words on the screen but also when you're reading corrections from your editor or engaging with living, breathing people or facing opportunities to act on those beliefs you wrote so passionately about.

If you're an actor, you can be a person of integrity not just secretly, when you're at home with your adoring family, but also when you're deciding whether to accept a project that would force you to use vulgar language or denigrate other people or put yourself in a compromising situation.

If you're a salesperson, you can be a person of integrity not just behind the safety of your closed office door but also when you're being asked to protect a confidence or negotiating with a cutthroat client or filling out your expense report and finding yourself tempted to blur the lines.

If you work retail, you can be a person of integrity not just when things are humming along but also when you're dealing with a difficult customer or reconciling the cash drawer or responding to your manager when he or she asks you to stay late . . . again.

If you're a pastor, you can be a person of integrity not just when you're on stage teaching congregants who think you hung the moon but also when you're interacting with your spouse, who is a little frustrated by ministry's incessant demands on your time, or when you're in a counseling session with a troubled soul.

Whoever you are and whatever you do, wherever your body goes, it is *there* that you can offer yourself as a living sacrifice to God.

Dallas-based pastor Tony Evans did a chapel service for my team once and said, "Listen, I'm up here at this podium talking to you as a Christian. I'm a pastor, so you expect me to be coming at things from a Christian point of view. But guess what? When I go home, I'm a Christian husband and dad. When I pull into my driveway, I'm a Christian neighbor. When I go shopping, I'm a Christian consumer. Wherever I go, I'm a Christian there, first and foremost, before I'm anything else."

That thought has stayed with me to this day.

If you are a follower of Jesus, you are a follower of his at all times, in all places, under all circumstances. Your body is to be a living sacrifice to God, wherever that body of yours goes.

THE STRUGGLE IS REAL

In 1984, Coach Noll promoted me to the role of defensive coordinator, and at age twenty-eight, I was the youngest in the league. Because of Coach Noll's prowess—he had coached the team to four Super Bowls in the 1970s—and because I was young and according to the watching world had something to prove, I probably looked a little vulnerable to the veterans in my sport. But I was being trained in integrity, and those messages were burrowing into my mind and heart. I mean it: I was really buying into this way of living and wanted nothing to do with life on my own terms ever again.

Fast-forward to December 29, 1984, at what was then Mile High Stadium in Denver, Colorado. It was the day before the AFC divisional playoffs between the third-seed Steelers and John Elway's second-seed Broncos, and the winner would play Miami in the AFC Championship Game the following week. We were one of eight teams remaining in the Super Bowl chase, and we were getting ready for our final workout in the Denver stadium.

During practice, one of the technicians setting up the television feed said hello to me in passing and then went about his work. He and countless other techs had been on the field for hours by then, both when the Broncos had practiced and now, as our team was running through plays.

After practice the guy came up to me and said, "Good luck. We should have a great game tomorrow. And by the way, I saw one of their halfbacks, number 47, throwing the ball. He has a pretty good arm!"

I couldn't believe it. He'd just let me in on a trick play that Denver might use on us the next day.

As I rode back to our hotel on the bus, I was in a terrible quandary. I had information that could really help our team, but it was information I shouldn't have been given. I hadn't asked for this tip. I'd done nothing wrong to get it. But now that I had it, what was I supposed to do?

Shouldn't I tell my players to be alert when number 47 came into the game? Shouldn't I do everything in my power to give them the best chance to win? Didn't I owe it to them to set them up for success? Didn't I owe it to our staff, to our owner, to our city?

As a coach, I'd have been upset if I found out someone had tipped off our opponents. But wouldn't it be foolish to just sit on this useful tip?

I thought about it all night. In the end, do you know what the deciding factor was? It was that whisper. That small voice in my head reminding me of what Paul said in Romans 12:2. *Don't do what the world does,* I thought to myself. *Think differently.*

It was ill-gotten gain, and I knew it. I had to keep the trick play to myself.

During the second quarter the following day, number 47 did come into the game. As I was sitting in the press box, having already called the defense, I had a feeling of what was coming. Sure enough, the Broncos ran that play—a halfback pass—and it went for fifty-two yards, inside our ten-yard line. I had a sick feeling in my stomach. *What if they go in and score a touchdown that ends up being the difference in the game?* But wouldn't you know it, three plays later we intercepted an Elway pass that turned the momentum of the game completely around. We ended up winning 24–17 and advanced to the championship game.

Could I have justified sharing the information I'd inappropriately received? Yep. All day long.

But the only way I was able to put my head on my pillow

that night and sleep was by refusing to conform to the world. It was by giving integrity the win.

• • •

I don't know what line of work you're in or how temptations generally come your way, but I do know that the struggle to ignore integrity's call is prevalent and pervasive and real. You've got to pre-decide how you're going to respond to those temptations, or they will take you down every time. It's one thing to maintain integrity when everything is going your way. But to hold that posture when everything is coming against you? That's next-level spiritual maturity. It's maturity we should seek.

Lauren and I were talking not long ago about this very topic, and she reminded me of how agonizing it was when I got fired from the Bucs. It felt like we were being evicted from the city we loved. We both understood why the move was made, but understanding it didn't make it sit any better with us. Pain is painful every time.

We were reflecting on that entire ordeal, and she said, "But we praise God in good times and in bad, don't we? That's who we are. That's what we do."

She was absolutely right. We work hard to practice what we preach in good times and in bad, when life feels generous and when things seem bleak, when there's a surplus and when there's a struggle . . . at all times, in all places, under all circumstances. He's "God of the hills and valleys," we heard Tauren Wells sing at a concert recently.

He most certainly is.

I like that proverb where the writer asks God for two things: "Give me neither poverty nor riches," he says, "but give me only my daily bread" (Proverbs 30:8, NIV). Keep me on the path, he's saying, veering neither too far left nor too far right. He knows that having too little may make him desperate, tempted to do things he would never before have considered, just to meet his basic needs. But also true is that having too *much* might make him forget his need for God. Nice and easy down the middle . . . that's where we want to be.

IT'S NEVER TOO LATE TO GET RIGHT WITH GOD

As I wrote the last section, I was reminded of way too many people I've known in my life who didn't live "nice and easy down the middle" with God. In some cases, they never acknowledged God at all. In others, they couldn't seem to match what they did with the beliefs they professed. I liken both situations to a baseball player hitting a home run who is ruled out because while he was rounding the bases, strutting around the bend, index finger pointed meaningfully toward heaven, he failed to touch first base. Remember the verse Lauren quoted earlier about gaining the whole world and losing your soul?

It's that.

What a devastating thing, to get to the end of your life and realize that you never tagged first base.

Lauren and I saw this dynamic play out countless times in the NFL family, and it was tragic every time. Some bright, young, talented guy would enter the league with stars in his eyes. An average of three and a half years later, he'd be done— sometimes not just with football but with daily life. He couldn't manage the instant fame, the instant wealth, the instant success, and once his career had ended, he had no idea how to thrive. (I would remember Coach Noll's warning. *Don't make football your whole life. Find your purpose.* And that's something I repeated over and over to my players as well, but it didn't always sink in.) It's uncanny in its predictability: the things of this world simply cannot truly satisfy. We were created by God to be satisfied only by him, and when we go chasing after all the non-God options that are out there, we're only going to bear this truth out time and again. There's a reason Christ followers keep following Christ! It's because he's the only place where hope can be found.

These days, whenever I have the chance to speak to young players, I tell them the same thing those veteran Steelers told me many years ago: decide right now to be more serious about following Jesus than you are about anything else.

Be more serious about Jesus than you are about football.

And your stats.

And your biceps.

And your social media presence.

And hanging out with your friends.

And being a husband.

And being a dad.

Be more faithful to Jesus than you are to anyone or anything else, because when you're faithful to Jesus, really and truly *faithful*, those other things will take care of themselves.

. . .

Can I ask you a question? Does your walk match your talk? Do you say that you value things like honesty and integrity but then live your life in such a way that those beliefs get violated on a regular basis? Are you living as a broken individual instead of living whole?

It doesn't have to be this way.

Do you believe me?

It doesn't have to be this way for you.

You can know peace.

You can receive divine guidance.

You can quit looking over your shoulder all the time, wondering if you're going to get nailed for something you said or did.

And the best news is this: *it's never too late to get right with God.*

That's the truth. The thief hanging on the cross next to Jesus who was accepted into God's eternal presence *as he hung there dying* ought to be proof positive of what I'm saying here. It was not too late for him, and as long as you're still breathing, it will never be too late for you.

. . .

At a men's conference last April, I spoke with famed MLB right fielder Darryl Strawberry, who played seventeen seasons with New York's Mets and Yankees clubs. I know Darryl well and count him a friend. Though I'd heard his testimony many times before, I sat there slack-jawed for the entirety of his talk. Here was his opener, word for word: "I was a liar. I was a cheater. I was a womanizer. I was an alcoholic. I was a drug addict. I was a sinner. I was rich. I was famous. I was lost. But I was saved by grace."

The crowd went wild, and the guy was only ten seconds into his talk. The reaction was understandable to me. Think about it: What kind of shot at a functional life does a lying, cheating, womanizing, boozing drug addict have? Slim to none, at most. What's more, Darryl had grown up with a violently abusive father who told Darryl and his brothers that they'd never amount to anything. The baggage that kid was carrying by the time he reached the majors was enough to make anyone's shoulders slump. And from there, things just got worse.

For a time, anyway.

To hear Darryl describe it, God rocked his world. "He took me from the pit to the pulpit," he said, and knowing what I know about his story, that's about as true a statement as there could be. Desperation. Suicidal thoughts. Dope houses. A Florida prison. Darryl had spent way too much time dropping by places that he should have dropped from his life altogether. But each time, his wife, Tracy, would come bail him out, steer him home, and say to him for the millionth time, "Darryl, God has a plan for your life, and his plans for you are good."

"I waited patiently for the LORD," David wrote in Psalm 40:1-2 (NIV), "he turned to me and heard my cry. He lifted me out of the slimy pit, out of the mud and mire; he set my feet on a rock and gave me a firm place to stand."

Darryl had spent not months or years in that slimy pit David described but *decades*. Oh, how good it must have felt when he was set on that firm place at last. "I don't know why it took me so long to get here," Darryl said to the men in the audience that day as he shook his head and collected himself. "I don't know what took me so long. . . ."

Those are tough words to hear, aren't they?

Those words are laced with deep regret.

Let me give you some better words, words that Darryl himself spoke: "I wasn't always on fire for Jesus, but I'm *totally* on fire today."

You know what's true of something that is totally on fire? It's consumed—utterly and completely consumed.

That's integrity—that's it. It's when we are utterly and completely consumed by our relationship with Christ. We talk differently. We walk differently. We *live* differently. We stand firm on that place of conviction, a hymn of praise to God on our lips. And we do this not just when it's convenient. We do this all the time.

3

"LEAD ME, LORD"

Choose Prayer

Lauren

The conference call was supposed to begin at ten in the morning, Pacific time. I was just sure this was the correct start time, but when Tony and I logged into the conference line, nobody else was there. The project's organizer hadn't reached out to either of us to say that anything had changed, so we figured she was either running late or had gotten the time wrong herself. Tony and I waited, believing that she would log in any moment, but after ten minutes had passed, we knew our wires had somehow gotten crossed.

Tony and I were in Oregon that day, and I remember sitting at the table in the little kitchen, his phone still on speaker as we wondered when the call would begin. As it became evident that the call wasn't going to transpire as planned, we had some options before us. We could choose impatience. After all, we had a lot of to-dos to tackle, and those things weren't going to get done while we sat there idle.

We could choose frustration. With a family our size, it's no small thing for Tony and me to sort out the logistics to pull away for an hour to engage in a substantive conversation. Time is precious. We don't like wasting time.

We could fire off a text in anger.

In annoyance, we could make a mental note not to say yes to this person again.

Or we could choose a far more radical response.

We picked that last one, the far more radical one. The response we chose was prayer.

Now, I tell you that story not because it is earth-shattering in its scope or because the turn of events was wildly consequential in our lives. I tell it to you because of how very *ordinary* the whole thing was. We had a call scheduled, the call didn't start on time, somebody probably goofed—so what? I tell it to you because it is exactly here, in the ordinary, day-to-day twists and turns of our lives, that we must learn to reflexively pray.

· · ·

Two weeks after that inconsequential phone mishap, I got word from across the country in Pittsburgh that my sweet mom had been admitted to the hospital. "We think she may be in a coma," my sister told me, an update that lacked the necessary details my mind and heart craved.

For the entirety of my life, Doris Jeanette "Bird" Harris had been my greatest cheerleader, my most devoted mentor, my most consistent example of Christlikeness, and my number one bestie. Such a rock she had always been for me, and now it felt like that rock was crumbling within my grip. Nobody could tell me exactly what was going on with my mom, but because she was in her nineties and because of the vast distance separating Pennsylvania from Oregon, a sinking feeling settled in my chest and made it difficult to breathe.

You can imagine the options facing me with this deeply emotional situation at hand. I could have impulsively caught a flight and spent the next eight hours with my stomach in my throat and my hands wringing each other raw. I could have called the hospital and steamrolled my way into some better information. I could have texted some serious marching orders to my brothers and my sister—couldn't *someone* get control over this situation?

Or I could choose a far more radical response.

I picked that last one, the radical one. The response I chose was prayer.

I tell you that story precisely because it *was* earth-shattering in its scope and because, in the moment, it felt like everything was hanging in the balance. Bird was in a coma, as far as the EMTs could tell, and because they weren't sure what had caused her to slip from consciousness, they weren't entirely sure how to get her back. My one and only mom was in crisis, and I was thousands of miles away. It is also here, in the extraordinary circumstances of our lives, that we must learn to reflexively pray.

PRAY FIRST; PRAY ALWAYS

Over the years, countless people have asked me how Tony and I manage such a big family. As individuals moving through this life, you'd probably agree that it's challenging enough just to keep up with our own personal obligations—getting where we're supposed to be, when we're supposed to be there, with the correct supplies or gear, and so forth. Now, multiply that by eleven kids, and you see where things get messy. In a given day, there are hundreds of decisions that must be made, dozens of accommodations that need to be arranged, and one giant truckload of logistical considerations to sort out. It's a lot. A *lot*, a lot.

Add to that mix the fact that most of our children are not ours biologically, which means we have to factor in the needs, obligations, and preferences of a dozen or so *other* adults, and things really get fun.

How do we do it, then? I'll give you the same one-word answer I always give: *prayer*. At the start of every single day, Tony and I pray for insight. We pray for courage. We pray for wisdom. We pray for peace. We praise God for being faithful to us and for his goodness throughout the earth. We thank him for the redemptive things he's up to in the world at large and in each Dungy's life.

We claim his forgiveness for the selfish or neglectful actions of the previous day and ask for his empowerment to lead righteous lives going forward. We bring the Lord every decision, every meeting, every obligation the coming day holds—the ones we know about, anyway—and ask for his divine guidance. There's the verse that says that God, "who did not spare his own Son, but gave him up for us all" will "graciously give us all things" (Romans 8:32, NIV).

How I love that promise! Tony and I choose to take God at his word that when we ask for things that are in alignment with his will, God will grant us those requests every time. And so we ask. Every day, we ask.

"Do we go to that doctor's appointment together, or should one of us stay home with the little kids?"

"How is [our son] Jordan's heart this morning, God? Is he doing all right? He seemed quiet yesterday. . . ."

"How is Jade going to get to work on time if she's watching little Kallie this afternoon for us?"

"What do we need to do to prepare for that discussion with our publisher this afternoon? Lord, who are you hoping to reach with this latest book project?"

"Should I say yes to helping with that new women's study at church, or do you have something else for me this month, Lord?"

"How can we come alongside our friends whose son keeps getting into trouble? We're supposed to see them tonight. What questions should we ask? How can we help them to feel seen and loved by you?"

Before our feet even hit the floor each morning, these are the words that are on our lips. "Guide us, Lord. Direct us, Lord. Empower us, Lord. Use us, Lord." At six o'clock, nine mornings out of ten, you'll find us still huddled under the covers, eyes open and minds humming, a whisper of fervent prayers the only sound in the room. We pray before we use the bathroom. We pray before we brush our teeth or hair. (Well, before *I* brush *my* hair, anyway.) We pray before we shower and get dressed. We pray before the hot tea gets made. We pray *before anything else* each morning because we so desperately need to hear from God.

By the time our day is underway, Tony and I are both clear

about what God has asked us to do. We have heard from our heavenly Father and are in agreement on our plan of attack, so we can step into our responsibilities with confidence, knowing we're not shooting from the proverbial hip. Then, as we face unexpected situations—and don't those always rear their ugly heads!—we persist in prayer, knowing that while we might feel sideswiped, God in heaven is not surprised. Proverbs 2:6-8 says that the Lord "gives wisdom; from his mouth come knowledge and understanding. He holds success in store for the upright, he is a shield to those whose walk is blameless, for he guards the course of the just and protects the way of his faithful ones" (NIV).

Wow. Such encouragement there is in that passage! Whenever life throws us a curveball, we can simply head right back to God in prayer and ask how to course-correct. Astoundingly, he then gives us wisdom, just like that proverb says. He gives us knowledge. He gives us understanding. He helps us factor in the unexpected and move forward in confidence and peace. In 1 Thessalonians 5:14-22, the apostle Paul rattled off a slew of things that believers do if they want to be set apart for God's use in the world and kept blameless until Jesus' return, and in the middle of that litany, he wrote, "pray continually" (NIV). Another version of the Bible translates this verse "pray without ceasing" (1 Thessalonians 5:17, NKJV).

Pray continually. Pray without ceasing. Pray as you go about your day. Pray, pray, pray, pray, pray. This is one of the key choices that Tony and I have made to stay softhearted and humble before God.

. . .

I've given a lot of thought to what prayer is over the four-plus decades that I've been walking with Jesus. How should we think about prayer? How would we define the idea, if asked? At the risk of oversimplifying a deeply spiritual concept, I will tell you that my definition of prayer has been whittled down over the years to four words: for me, prayer is *conscious connection with God*. If God's Spirit is living inside us—and he is for all who have surrendered their lives to God—then you could say we are always "connected with God." But we often neglect to acknowledge that connection, to intentionally talk with him and invite his presence to permeate our hours each day. When we pray, we *consciously* connect with God. We turn from our own whims and ask what's on his mind. We turn from our own will and ask what he desires. We turn from our own ways and ask what he's up to in the world.

Conscious connection with God—that's it. That's what prayer has become for me. And in my view, there is no greater resource this side of heaven than consciously staying connected to God. That connection is what gives me hope during desperate situations. It's what gives me a sense of peace when chaos reigns. It's what provides perspective when I'm fixated on a microscopic detail of life that refuses to fall within my control. It's my on-ramp to right thinking, right living, when I seem to be getting life wrong.

And yet I'm just as likely as the next person to neglect this beautiful exchange called prayer. Uncanny, isn't it?

What I'd like to do in the balance of this chapter is to lay out for you three reminders I constantly offer myself, to keep on prioritizing prayer. Here's a sneak peek: *Prayer is easy. Prayer is hard.* And finally, *Prayer is best.*

Let's take each one in turn.

PRAYER IS EASY

If my memory serves me well, I was six years old when I prayed my first prayer. I wouldn't make a volitional decision to surrender my life to Jesus until I was nineteen, but given the values in the Harris household, prayer was just "what we did." As I recall, Bird was frying chicken on the stove while at the same time trying to get my brother ready for a birthday party he was going to attend. She was multitasking, and while all the current research tells us that it's literally impossible to tend to more than one task, what mom hasn't been tempted to try? With five kids running around at all times, Bird was perpetually juggling a dozen balls, and this day was no different. I wasn't in the kitchen when the explosion happened, but as I rushed toward the jolting sound, I could tell that somehow the vat of boiling grease had splashed onto my mom's exposed face. Someone had the presence of mind to call 911, and it couldn't have been two minutes before screaming sirens neared and my mom was being loaded onto a stretcher and raced to the nearest hospital.

I was terrified. I remember sinking to the carpeted floor in the living room, completely stunned by what I'd seen. I sobbed and sobbed. What had happened to my mom? Where had they taken her? Would she be okay? A thousand questions flooded my little mind, vying for attention, begging for answers that simply couldn't be found.

All the adults who had rushed over during the ambulance commotion began frantically talking, speculating, and strategizing, and while I was eager to learn whatever they knew of the situation, all I could do was pray.

Isn't it funny how our memories work? I'd been surrounded by believers my entire life but hadn't yet made the decision to surrender my life to Jesus, yet intuitively I knew I needed help in that moment that only Jesus could provide. There, from the living room floor, I cried out to God. "God, if you're there, I need to tell you something," I said to the heavens, praying aloud as my grandmother and mother always did. "Bird is hurt. She is hurt real bad. Would you please help her? She has been burned and is probably in so much pain. Please help her, God. Please tell the doctors how to fix her. Please help her not be afraid."

Looking back, I can see how totally natural it was for me to pray that prayer instantaneously and reflexively and from the heart. As a kid, I saw my grandmother pray to God all the time. We'd be wandering the grocery store aisles, shopping for the week ahead, and she'd stop right there in the middle of the place and talk to God for four or five minutes straight. We'd be heading off somewhere in the car, and before she pulled out, she'd sit there in the driver's seat with her eyes closed, petitioning God. I'd see her chatting with a neighbor in the backyard, and before I knew it, Nana would grab that neighbor's hand, tilt her head skyward, and offer up a prayer on the neighbor's behalf. For my grandmother, prayer was the easiest possible thing to do. What was more natural than prayer?

. . .

These days, I'd have to agree with my grandmother: What's more natural than prayer? When you like someone, you want to talk with that person, right? Communicating with someone you like is the most natural thing in the world. When you like someone, you're curious to know more. And how will you truly learn about that person than through communication with him or her? The same is true for prayer. If we like God, then we'll like *talking* with God. We'll be curious to know what he's thinking, what he's doing—and asking him is how we'll find out.

As it turned out, my mom would need to spend many months in the hospital to heal from that horrific kitchen accident, and her absence was every bit as disruptive to our family as you'd assume. I couldn't have known it at the time, but God used those tumultuous months to carve out a deep capacity in me for the discipline of prayer. I was only a child, but through that experience, God formed in me a spiritual maturity that serves me still today. In the most basic terms, here's what happened: I knew enough about God to understand that he was in control of the world, and given how upended my world had become, I desperately wanted his insights into what was going on. Because I knew that he had the answers to every question, I wanted to talk to him. I wanted to hear from him. I wanted to lay out my concerns and have him address them, one by one.

So there was that: I was curious. I wanted to know what he knew. I wanted more information than I had at the time. I wanted to see what only he saw. But there was more, because over time I realized that the more I talked with God, the more I wanted to talk with God. My motivation may have been somewhat selfish at first—"Is Bird going to make it, God? Tell me! Tell me, please!"—but after a while, I prayed not to get something from God but rather just to be with God. As days bled into weeks and weeks turned into months, prayer became a soft place for me to land when everything in life felt hard.

Priscilla Shirer, one of my favorite authors on the subject of prayer, says that "experiencing the manifest presence of God doesn't satisfy your hunger; it only whets your appetite for more."[1] And while at six years of age, I certainly couldn't have articulated my feelings with that level of eloquence or poignance, I believe that Priscilla's sentiment was absolutely true for me back then.

Prayer begets prayer, and as a child I couldn't get enough.

And then there was this: the more faithful I was in coming to God with my concerns and listening quietly for his subtle response, the more connected I felt to him. A certain intimacy was blooming between us, even though it would be years before I'd trust him with my life. (It's worth noting that by the time I did surrender to Jesus, I felt as though we were old friends.)

Prayer was *easy* for me back then. And prayer *remains easy* for me now. What's easier, more natural, than prayer? If God designed us and created us—and you well know that I believe he did—then wouldn't the act of talking with him be almost second nature? Think of it: you don't have to dial any phone numbers or send any texts. You don't have to snap a photo and post a long caption. You don't have to launch into any lengthy explanations or recap your version of the story. You don't have to worry about whether your good news will make someone jealous or your bad news will bring someone down. You don't have to stay stuck in fear or anxiety or confusion. You can simply—*easily*—pray. You can stop what you're doing, quiet your mental hamster wheel, and pray.

You can ask for help from the One who longs to assist you.

You can request insight from the One who knows all.

You can beg for wisdom from the One who invented it.

You can be steadied in the space of a single exhale.

You can talk with God—the Creator of the entire universe—and be set right once more. What you don't see, he sees. What you don't hear, he perceives. What you don't know, he knows. What you don't understand, he grasps. He is above all. He is below all. He surrounds all and hems us in. He is within all and through all and is the One who sustains all of everything. And we can gain access to him through prayer.

If there is anything easier than turning to our infinite, all-knowing, all-seeing, all-present God whenever we need encouragement, insight, or peace, I can't for the life of me think what that would be.

There is nothing easier than prayer. And yet the conversation does not end there.

PRAYER IS HARD

Here's a second reminder I offer myself pretty much every day: *Prayer is hard.* I know, I know. We just spent several pages talking about why prayer is the easiest imaginable thing. It *is* easy—I'm sticking to my story there. And also: prayer is *hard.*

Prayer is hard because of what we must give if we hope to be committed to the prayerful way of life. Prayer takes time. Prayer takes energy. Prayer takes focus. And sometimes, especially when we're hit with a stressful set of circumstances, the last thing we want to do or think we're *capable* of doing is to pull away and train our attention on our heavenly Father. It's so hard to redirect our energies from stressing over the disaster in front of us to trusting God for something promising to rise from those ashes. Left to our nature, you and I and every other human to walk this planet suffer from a strong negativity bias that finds it far more desirable to think about negative events than positive ones. Asking us to let go of our fussing and fretting and fixating is like asking a dog to drop the bone that is presently clamped in his locked jaws.

Years ago, we hired a workman to come to our home and clean out our gutters. He was probably seventy years old, and I remember thinking how fortunate we were to have such an experienced professional helping us out. He'd done roofing work for more than five decades and had "seen it all," he said. I felt like we were in good hands.

What neither he nor I could have predicted was that on that day, for whatever reason, his vast experience easing along rooftops failed him, and he took a wild tumble from the roof of our house onto the pavement below. The kids were outside playing when it happened, so within moments, they alerted me to the tragic fall. Once I learned that paramedics had already been called, I rushed over to the man, who was still lying on the ground moaning in pain. Years of reflexive praying determined my next move. "Do you mind if I pray for you?" I asked, to which he nodded slightly. I proceeded to pray heaven down on behalf of that man, I have to tell you. I didn't know him. I didn't know his family. I didn't yet know the severity of his situation. I didn't know what would become of this terrible turn of events. But I knew One who did, and you'd better believe that I wasted no time in bringing the situation before God.

Once the man had been transported to the hospital and given a favorable report—miraculously, if you ask me—I revisited my prayerful response. Should I have at least tried to engage him in conversation or gotten him some ice or something before asking if I could pray for him? Should I have just prayed silently while going about more demonstrably helpful tasks instead of forcing him to listen to me pray? What if he didn't know God? What if he didn't like God? What if I offended him somehow while he was lying there on my driveway, writhing in pain?

The Lord himself soothed my conscience with an insight I remember to this day: there is no better way to spend a minute of time, a calorie of energy, or a synapse of focus than in prayer with almighty God. Isn't that a comforting truth? There is not a single thing you could do to better steward your time, energy, or focus than to invest it in communicating with God. And yet sometimes, upon making those investments, you're going to feel wasteful, or foolish, or wrong. Which is when you'll need to remember what I've told you: *there's no better investment than prayer*.

I hold fast to that comforting truth when I labor in long-term prayer. Recently, a dear friend and her husband adopted a child whom my prayer-warrior friends and I had been praying about daily for two and a half years. We would pray and pray and pray, and then a birth mom would change her mind. We'd all pray and pray and pray some more, and then another adoptive family would be chosen instead of our friend. We'd pray and pray and pray yet again, and governmental red tape would tangle the whole deal. Nearly *three years* of this, until finally that baby came home. Where was God? What was he doing? Why was this taking so long? I may never know the answers to those questions, but of this much I am sure: *there is not a single thing we could have been doing to better steward our time, energy, or focus than investing it in communication with God.*

I hold fast to that comforting truth when I don't particularly like the answer I receive from God. Last year, a friend told me that her son was running for state-level office and sent me his campaign website. She was clearly proud of the turn of events and wanted me to rejoice, but when I read through the site, I noticed that perhaps in an effort to attract additional voters, her son had wavered on an aspect of God's truth. I prayed about the situation, wondering how to be supportive of my dear friend. I hoped that God would simply ask me to exhibit greater compassion for my friend and for her son, but that's not at all what he said. Instead, he prompted me to approach my friend and ask her explicitly about the content I'd seen on her son's site. "Are you sure, God?" I asked. (I *really* didn't want to go there.)

It was almost as if God responded, "Daughter, you do what you wish. But if you're asking for *my* thoughts on the situation, I think I've been pretty clear. . . ."

As I picked up the phone to call my friend, I thought, *The best possible thing I can do with my time and energy is to spend it communicating with God.* I'd prayed. And based on what I'd heard in prayer, I knew my action was in line with God's will.

I also hold fast to that comforting truth when I am granted the exact desire of my heart. I feel immense gratitude when I ask God for peace and receive it or ask God for clarity and receive it or ask God for hope and receive it. As a loving Father, he adores giving good gifts to his children. Whenever God bestows upon my life a very good gift, I am reminded that there is no better investment I can make than sitting and talking with him.

• • •

Yes, prayer is hard because of what we must *give:* time, energy, focus—and often, significant quantities of each. But prayer is also hard because of what we must *give up.* Prayer demands that we give up control.

I don't know if this rings true for you, but I rather like control. Given the pandemic we've recently lived through and what it revealed about how much control we actually have in this world, perhaps I should recast that sentence and say that I rather like the *illusion* of control. I like to have a plan, and I like to work that plan. I like to order my family's days and feel prepared for what those days will include. I enjoy that feeling of anticipating needs and meeting them with room to spare. I like being *ready* for life, which is sort of a problem for one who also values prayer.

At one point during Jesus' earthly ministry, his disciples asked him to teach them how to pray. In what has become known as the Sermon on the Mount, a series of passages in which Jesus explained to his followers how to be believers in a world that had little use for the things of God, Jesus answered their request and gave instructions on prayer. He shared some general counsel—don't pray to be seen by others, don't babble about nothing in your prayers—then gave them an actual script. "This, then, is how you should pray," he said in Matthew 6:9 (NIV), and offered up what became known as the Lord's Prayer.

That famous prayer starts, "Our Father in heaven, hallowed be your name, your kingdom come, your will be done, on earth as it is in heaven" (vv. 9-10, NIV).

Did you notice that *our* kingdom isn't mentioned, and that *our* will is nowhere to be found?

It can be difficult to forfeit our preferences and desires in the moment, but the promise of God is that as we conform ourselves to his will and ways instead of asking him to conform to ours, we will enjoy more and more what he calls "life that is truly life" (1 Timothy 6:19, NIV). It is this kind of life that you and I desire. And when we're tempted to go our own way, we must remember that it's a form of life found only in God.

I know it's popular today to try to define truth on our own terms. There is plenty of messaging in our world that tells us to live according to what pleases us and to chart our own course instead of surrendering to anyone or anything. While I trust that the message bearers promoting this line of thinking are trying to appear accepting and tolerant, the reality is that two opposing definitions of truth can't both be true. If what you deem truthful contradicts what I deem truthful, then we need an arbiter to step in and rule on the situation. We need Someone who sees more broadly than we do to tell us who is right.

That Someone, of course, is God.

The prophet Isaiah recorded God's perspective on our ability to be the arbitrator in Isaiah 55:8-9 (NIV): "'For my thoughts are not your thoughts, neither are your ways my ways,' declares the LORD. 'As the heavens are higher than the earth, so are my ways higher than your ways and my thoughts than your thoughts.'"

Sure, we can keep pushing for our own thoughts to be the arbiters of truth and for our own ways to be the ways that others follow, but if *higher* thoughts and *higher* ways are available, wouldn't we be wise to check them out? If we could have an uncommon influence in our generation instead of settling for that which is common, wouldn't we want to do everything in our power to seal that deal?

The hard part of prayer: ceding control. The beautiful part that follows that hard part: higher thoughts and higher ways.

I take the trade every time.

. . .

A third and final reason that prayer is hard is this: an opponent seeks to disrupt our intimacy with God.

Scripture describes Satan as a roaring lion who prowls the earth, looking for someone to devour (see 1 Peter 5:8). He is called the father of lies (see John 8:44). He is called our accuser (see Revelation 12:10). And he is called the deceiver of the whole world (see Revelation 12:9). In short, he's not on our side. He isn't out for our good. He doesn't have our best interest at heart. Something else that is true of him is that he absolutely hates it when we pray.

Whenever someone endeavors to deepen their intimacy with God, Satan and his minions cringe. Enjoying intimate connection with our heavenly Father means experiencing wisdom and light and life. And for one who exists in eternal darkness, nothing is worse than the light. Which, I believe, is why every time you or I try to sit down in silence and pray, the phone rings. Or the lightbulb in the lamp goes out. Or the dog starts barking. Or a delivery person rings the bell.

I'm kidding.

But only partially.

I'm not sure that Satan himself is behind any of the daily distractions we face when trying to pray, but I do know that our devotion to the practice of prayer is an outright annoyance to him. He would much prefer that our minds stay blinded, that our hearts stay hard, that our affections stay worldly, and that our actions stay self-centered. He would much prefer that we quit giving a whit about someone else's struggles and that we quit being curious about how God might want us to be part of the solution to the problems we see. He is surely elated every time we neglect to pray.

This is why in the first part of this chapter I described my choice to pray as a "radical" decision. According to the apostle Paul's words in Ephesians 6, each time we decide to pray, we willingly insert ourselves right in the middle of the spiritual battle for our very souls by taking our stand against the devil's schemes (see v. 11). Paul said to "put on the full armor of God, so that when the day of evil comes, you may be able to stand your ground, and after you have done everything, to stand" (v. 13, NIV).

He went on to detail each piece of that armor—the belt of truth, the breastplate of righteousness, the shoes of the gospel of peace, the shield of faith, the helmet of salvation, and the sword of the Spirit (vv. 14-17)—and then, in closing, he said to pray. "*Pray* in the Spirit on all occasions with all kinds of prayers and requests," he wrote. "*Keep on praying* for all the Lord's people" (v. 18, emphasis mine).

Pray.

Keep on praying.

It's how the battle gets won.

Which brings me to the final truth I want to offer you. Despite how hard prayer can sometimes feel, *prayer is always best*.

PRAYER IS BEST

I don't have to tell you that life in this fallen world is tough stuff. Disappointment awaits us daily, doesn't it? Everywhere we turn, we see someone struggling—and many times, that person is us. Things happen to us that break our hearts into a thousand pieces. Friends betray us. Family members say hurtful things. Neighbors don't act very neighborly. Pastors fall from grace. Parents skip out on court dates where weighty decisions will be made regarding the children they do, in fact, love. This world can be a burdensome place. The problems. The challenges. The heartache. The pain. It's no wonder God calls his children to prayer. He's known all along what we are sometimes slow to accept: we simply can't face this life alone. We need his wisdom, direction, perspective, and faithful counsel. We need his gift of prayer. And so, regardless of how you're feeling in a given moment, may I gently exhort you to pray?

Pray early. Pray before your feet hit the floor in the morning. You might commit this phrase to memory: "Pray, then day." Pray. Then go about your day. Welcome the Lord's presence as you wake to the day he has made. Thank him for his mercies, which Scripture says are new every single day (see Lamentations 3:23). Bless his name for his wondrous works, and then cite a few of those works specifically. Has he blessed you with a comfortable home to live in? Has he given you a car to drive? Has he put loving family members around you? Has he directed you to a thriving church? Thank him for these wild blessings! So many people in the world would give anything for even one of the vast blessings you enjoy.

Walk through the day ahead with your Father, leaving no detail out. Did you know that God delights in the details of our lives? He does. He loves to hear your heart. To hear your concerns. To hear your plans. As you tell him these details, ask for his input at every turn. What might he want you to say in a particular meeting? How might he want you to encourage that neighbor you tend to see whenever you walk the dog? Does your spouse need something that you can help provide? Is there a burden you might help lift?

I can think of no better way to begin a day than in conversation with God. Try it tomorrow—I dare you. You might just become a fan.

Yes, yes: pray early. And then, *pray often*. Steal secret moments throughout your day—while waiting at a stoplight, while putting gas in your car, while waiting in the carpool line, while walking to get the mail—to ask God where he's at work in your corner of the world. "What am I not seeing this afternoon, Father?" you might ask him. "Who would you like to bring to my mind?"

I know that it's easy to become distracted by our own burdens, our own struggles, our own terribly long to-do lists, but I promise you that if you commit yourself to praying to be used by God, God will supernaturally tend to the weightiness you once bore. Trust him in this. He longs to take that heaviness, exchanging it for a burden he says is light (see Matthew 11:30).

Next, *pray alone*. We see plenty of evidence in Scripture of Jesus slipping away from the crowds to spend time with his Father alone. In fact, the Gospel writer Luke was careful to include this detail about him: "Jesus often withdrew to lonely places and prayed" (Luke 5:16, NIV).

In order to maintain intimacy with Tony, I must carve out time when he and I can enjoy each other's company without a bunch of children running around. In the same way, if you and I expect to enjoy intimacy with God, we simply must pull away from time to time—"often," as Luke said of Jesus—and sit in his presence, alone.

Pray alone . . . and also, *pray with others*. Some of my favorite memories with family and friends are of times when we joined together in prayer. I love sitting around the dinner table praying the "ABCs of God" with my kids: "God is *A*ble! God is *B*eautiful! God is *C*aring! God is *D*evoted to our growth! God is *E*ncouraging! . . ."

I love praying with Tony for our kids' future spouses and future children.

I love meeting up with my running group to tackle an exhausting park route—and knowing that each time we spot someone sitting on one of the many park benches dotting the path, a few of us will hang back. We'll walk toward that person, introduce ourselves, chat for a few moments, and ask how we can pray for him or her.

I love watching each child we foster start to engage in our evening family prayers. They are always shy at first, saying "Pass" when it's their turn to pray. But over time—sometimes in a matter of days—they are nearly bouncing out of their seats with eagerness to join in.

I love hearing from neighborhood parents that our kids always want to excuse themselves from playing with their friends to get home in time for those pre-bedtime family prayers. If God is going to speak, they don't want to miss it! Who can blame them for that?

I love the incredible luxury of group-texting my five fellow prayer warriors when I need their intercession, and I love the honor of praying for them when they're the ones who hit Send.

I love seeing my kids owning the power of prayer for themselves. These days, for example, when I drive by a car accident with kids in my car, I can look in the rearview mirror and catch some of them quietly closing their eyes to pray for those who were involved in the wreck.

I love connecting in person with my Thursday afternoon

prayer group and seeing how God answers our requests week after week after week.

Listen, if you're reading these examples and thinking, *I sure wish I had someone to pray with,* let that request be your prayer. Ask God to send you a prayer partner, someone who will practice the discipline of prayer with you, who will keep you accountable in praying consistently, and who will be honored to uphold you in prayer as needs arise. God loves to answer this prayer because God loves it when we pray.

And finally, regarding what to pray, consider *structured prayers.* There are lots of wonderful formats online that you could start with, but perhaps the best-known is referred to as "A.C.T.S." (Google "ACTS prayer format," and you'll be handed five million wonderful ideas.) In short, you begin your prayer with *Adoration,* telling God how wonderful he is and how faithful he's been in your life. Next, move to *Confession* by claiming God's forgiveness for the ways you've missed the mark. First John 1:9 says that when we mess up, God stands ready to forgive us, if only we will agree with him about the sinful thing we did. Waste no time confessing your sin! Freedom waits for you on the other side.

Third, enter a time of *Thanksgiving,* during which you express gratitude for the blessings in your life. Conclude your time with *Supplication,* which is a fancy word for "prayer requests." Ask God for what you need—or think you need. Ask him to meet the needs of those struggling in your world. Then ask for the patience and complete surrender to accept his answers to your prayers.

Something else I enjoy doing is praying Scripture back to God. You might select a favorite psalm to pray, changing up the pronouns so you're speaking in the first person to him. You might pray a passage to him such as Ephesians 6, which we talked about earlier, by saying something like, "Father, I put on your armor this morning. I fasten the belt of truth around me: I want to walk in the truth today. I put on the breastplate of righteousness: I ask you to direct my steps so that I take the path of righteousness at every turn. I fit the gospel of peace to my feet: help me to be a peacemaker today in every conversation I have."

I could keep going with that passage, but I think you get the idea.

Or what about Philippians 4:6? Tell God, "I choose not to worry about anything today, Father! Instead, I will bring my concerns to you in prayer all day long."

Prayers like that probably delight the heart of our Father in ways we'll never understand. We know that the Bible is the Word of God, inspired by him alone. Imagine how gratifying it must be to hear his children repeating his words back to him in prayer.

In the same breath that I tell you to pray structured prayers—which include prayers of saints from long ago, prayers of Scripture that God wrote, prayers that fit into something of a formula such as "A.C.T.S."—I will also tell you to *pray free-form prayers*. I can't tell you how often I pause whatever I'm doing, shake my head in wonder over the beautiful life God has given me, and say, "Father, you are so good to me. Thank you for your goodness, Lord."

I encourage you to do the same. Tell him hello. Tell him thank you. Tell him how blessed you feel. What a gift to return to him unprompted throughout your day, again and again and again.

In short, *pray*. Pray first and pray often. Pray alone and in the company of others. Pray structured prayers and free-form prayers. Just *be sure to continuously pray*. Pray because you love God's company. Pray because you want to know him more. Pray because you want to become more like him. Pray because you understand that he longs to hear from you and that he is eager to respond.

A LEGACY OF PRAYER

One morning recently, my adult son Jordan and I were talking about all that the day held for our family, and within about three minutes, it became evident to us both that there simply weren't enough hours in the day to do everything that needed to be done and get everyone where they needed to go. Tony was out of town, so we were down a driver, and just as I was about to panic, Jordan said, "Well, we'd better pray."

If you have a child, then you know that as parents, we can craft quite a list of goals for our kids. We can get pretty wrapped up in their various interests and start attaching ourselves to their academic or athletic or vocational outcomes, pushing them ever harder to achieve, achieve, achieve. And yet if you were to ask me to cut that list down to the single most important outcome in a child's life, it would have nothing to do with outward accomplishments. In my view, the single greatest outcome we ought to desire for our children is that they would cultivate and hold fast to the unparalleled practice of prayer. Good grades, sports trophies, and having a rewarding job are fine, but for real impact, your child is going to need real power. Supernatural power. The power that is found in God alone.

Good grades won't help your child stand firm against Satan's schemes for him or her.

Sports trophies won't help your child move successfully through a season of grief after losing a loved one.

A beloved profession can be a marvelous part of life, but in terms of facilitating wholesale transformation, it's going to take more than that.

What I'm saying is that a very real byproduct of prioritizing prayer is that by God's grace your children will start prioritizing prayer too. Which someday will influence *their* children to prioritize prayer. That's how it happened for me, anyway. My grandmother was about as faithful a prayer warrior as the world ever saw. My mama caught the vision and devoted herself to prayer as well. Even as a six-year-old, I grasped that prayer was an effective way to respond to crises, and so that fire was set ablaze inside of me, too. Tony and I look at our kids and see that their desire to pray was formed in large part because *we* have the desire to pray. You can get an awful lot wrong in parenting, yet if you fan into flame the earnest desire to pray in your child's heart, I'd say job well done.

• • •

Last month, during a visit to Bird in Pittsburgh, I saw her beautiful face for what would be my final time. My daughter Jade, my sister Amanda, and I were sitting at her bedside, holding her hands, gazing into her loving eyes when she transitioned into glory, and as tears streamed down my cheeks, I praised God that I hadn't missed that staggering moment.

A whole series of events had unfolded following the hospital admittance months before that were devastating to watch. But I have to tell you that despite my deep pain over saying goodbye to my earthly guiding light, as I spoke with my mom one last time, I was flooded with a tremendous wave of peace. My mom's greatest influence in my life was introducing me to Jesus—her Savior, her hero, her friend. And while I was decidedly *not* thrilled about the prospect of facing the coming days, weeks, months, and years without Bird's sweet voice cheering me on, because of my ability to access this Jesus who saw all and knew all and cared for all, I knew I'd be okay.

In teaching me to pray, Bird had taught me where to find hope. Where to find peace. Where to find joy when sorrow fell all around me like rain. I could be encouraged, no matter my circumstances. I could be strengthened, and I could be helped. I could face whatever the day might hold because I knew how to—and chose to—pray.

The same is true for you, you know.

If you will make the choice to pray.

4

READY TO ROLL

Choose to Prepare

Tony

I've coached hundreds of men across my career and have played with hundreds more, and never have I encountered someone who upheld the value of preparation more than NFL Hall of Famer Peyton Manning. A story comes to mind. We were two weeks out from Super Bowl XLI, and we would spend the first week practicing at home in Indianapolis before heading down to Miami the week of the game. Peyton came up to me at the beginning of practice one day and said, "Hey, Coach, I was looking at the fourteen-day forecast down in Miami, and it's gonna rain."

"Yeah?" I said, thinking but not saying that in the Super Bowl's four-decade history, not once had it ever rained during a game. It had been windy during some games. It had been really, really cold in one early Super Bowl in New Orleans. (Score for them. It's probably why they got their domed stadium.) But rain? Never once. Who knows why, but rain and Super Bowls just don't mix. I'd played in a Super Bowl in Miami. I couldn't picture it raining on Super Bowl Sunday. And by the way, with all the tape he'd been watching and scouting reports he'd been poring over, when did he have time to look at the fourteen-day forecast? Nah, it would be a warm, sunny day at Dolphin Stadium on February 4, 2007.

"Yeah," Peyton continued. "Coach, I think we'd better practice with wet balls."

The suggestion shouldn't have surprised me. This was Peyton Manning, the guy who came to every weekly team meeting with a yellow legal pad containing five to six hand-written single-spaced pages of fresh ideas for how best to face our next competitor. Undoubtedly, he had watched more film than anyone else—coaches included. I know this because he insisted on having our A/V guys pipe in footage to the top-of-the-line home theater he'd built for that very purpose. While other players were vegging out on the couch at 9 p.m. watching *24* or *The Shield* or *ER*, Peyton was studying every game the Bears had played for the last two years, noting every nuance of their approach.

Also true was that Peyton Manning had what I presumed was a divinely inspired gift for absorbing, assimilating, and retaining information. The combination of his God-given talent and his unwavering devotion to preparedness at any cost made him a force to be reckoned with—not only on the field but every day of the year. "He's always been this way," his parents told me one time: always observing, always scrutinizing, always strategizing, always looking for the edge.

"I'll give you three," I used to always tell Peyton. He knew what that meant, which is why the comment always elicited a grimace. I'd pick three of his scores of yellow-pad game-prep ideas, and as a team we'd implement those. The rest, he'd have to bag.

I probably don't have to tell you that on February 4, 2007, history was made. For the first time in Super Bowl history, it rained on game day. Not just rained but *poured*. Google it. It was the first rainy Super Bowl ever played.

It's a good thing I listened to him on this one and had our equipment men break out those wet balls for practice. We all need a Peyton Manning close by. Life works better when you're prepared.

. . .

In football, it's said that you perform like you prepare. Prepare effectively, and your performance reflects it every time. "Perfect preparation makes for perfect performance," I'd often tell the team, and while it wasn't ever possible to hit the perfection mark, by aiming for perfect preparation, we'd catch excellence along the way. Excellence has always been good enough for me. Excellence wins games.

Twelve years ago, I transitioned into my broadcast role with NBC and found that preparation matters greatly there, too. There are weekly planning calls to map out our team's top three or four storylines. Countless emails and scripts flying our way day after day that need to be reviewed, edited, responded to. Debrief video calls a few days after each airing with the executive producer and the producer to hear what we got right and what we could have done better. Endless online articles regarding the goings-on in the NFL. Cumulatively, it takes a lot of time. Our preparation is never complete.

Now, our show is a full ninety minutes long, but if I were to pull just the clips that involve my talking—either directly to the camera or to my colleagues Mike Tirico and Drew Brees— the total running time would be less than fifteen minutes. In anticipation of those fifteen minutes each week, I probably put in fifteen *hours* of prep. It's a wild ratio, yet if I had even more time to invest in getting ready for Sunday night, I'd happily invest it. The last thing I want to do is turn up unprepared. Same was true during my coaching days. The rest of the coaching staff and I would log fifty or sixty hours in preparation for each matchup—twelve to fourteen hours on Monday, Tuesday, and Wednesday, ten on Thursday, another six on Friday, maybe two or three each Saturday—and *still* there were weeks when we felt less than ready for the game.

When Lauren and I began discussing the scope of this book and the myriad lessons we've learned along the way regarding how to have uncommon influence in the world— something we pray is true of us, for sure—this theme of *preparation* kept popping up. We both grew up watching our parents prepare for their work, both their paid jobs and the service opportunities they seized. My mom and dad both were teachers, working with high school and college students. During the school year, it was normal for us to see them poring over their lesson plans at the kitchen table, making sure everything was just right, before heading off to bed. Two, three hours, they would sit there going over details, ordering their comments, nailing down the goal they planned to chase the next school day. Those are the memories of my parents

I carry with me still today. They cared deeply about the kids they were instructing. They cared enough to show up each morning ready to roll.

What my parents taught me early on was that the way people spend their time, their energy, their money—any of their resources, really—tells the world what they're preparing for. My parents spent their resources raising my siblings and me with compassion, grace, and love. They spent their resources faithfully shaping the lives of those schoolchildren. They spent their resources serving neighbors in need. They spent their resources helping out at church. To look at where their time, energy, and money went was to know that these people were *committed* to the way of Christ. They loved investing in education and personal growth. They loved investing in helping anyone who needed help. They loved investing in the art of leadership . . . and they were great leaders themselves. Those were crucial lessons for me during my formative years. Based on where I was pointing my energies, what was *I* preparing for?

Based on where you're investing your resources, what are *you* preparing for? Are your preparations pointing you toward an intentional goal, or have you started settling for being carried by the winds and whims of life?

Listen, I have given most of my adult life to a sport that, at its core, is a form of entertainment, so this is a judgment-free zone. But I will say this: if I couldn't use my platform with football to accomplish other, more important objectives than scoring a touchdown or talking about the guys who did, then I'd quit. I'd have quit long ago. Yes, I love this game. I loved playing it, I loved coaching it, and I love commenting on it all day, every day now. But there is something I love far more than football, and that is the person of Jesus Christ. And to the extent that being known as a football guy gives me opportunity to shine the light and love of Jesus to a world that can often feel dark and cast adrift, I count my mission complete.

This may sound crazy to you, but when I'm preparing for our broadcast, I'm not just thinking about the storyline we need to cover. I'm also thinking about how that story would be seen by Christ. How would he respond to the situation at hand? How would he look upon the people involved? What would he say to bring peace to the chaos? How might he use me to bring good news from bad?

So, on a typical Thursday morning, while it may seem on the surface like I'm just preparing for the big game the team and I are covering on Sunday night, what I'm actually doing is further preparation toward the man I hope to become.

. . .

For the rest of this chapter, I'd like to walk through three major preparations I feel like I'm constantly making toward becoming a person of uncommon influence. Lauren is making the same ones in the areas she's involved in. We believe that regardless of the course your life has taken or what you "do" day in and day out, these are preparations you, too, can make as you look to have an impact on your corner of the world. As Coach Noll used to tell us, "Champions don't do extraordinary things; they do the ordinary things better than anybody else."

In a way, this is an "ordinary things" sort of chapter. But if you stick to doing these three things well, you will absolutely win in life.

PREPARE TO LOVE

I've been asked on many occasions what I'm afraid of. Pretty common question, I suppose, and while as a Christ follower my standard answer is that we're told throughout Scripture *not* to fear, I'm human just like you. We probably both get afraid from time to time. The answer after my standard answer is this: I'm afraid for the future my children and grandchildren are going to have in this country called the United States of America unless we all get serious about uniting soon. There is more division in our country than I have seen in my six decades of living, and people older than I whom I deeply respect tell me the same is true for them. It seems every day we find a new reason to distance ourselves from some person or some group; instead of pulling in the same direction, we're racing off in a million different ones, fueled by anger, outrage, offense.

I trust God to be sovereign over all things—our seeming insistence on separation included. But if you want to know what keeps me up at night, it's that. It's disunity running its course.

The first preparation you and I simply must make, if we hope to have uncommon influence, is the preparation called *love*. This may sound pretty touchy-feely coming from a grid-iron guy, but hear me out: without love in our hearts, nothing else good can unfold. The apostle Paul wrote in his first letter to the believers at Corinth that if he "could speak all the languages of earth and of angels, but didn't love others," he "would only be a noisy gong or a clanging cymbal" (1 Corinthians 13:1)—in other words, annoying, if not impossible, to be around. I think you'd agree that to have uncommon influence, at a bare minimum, we should keep from gonging or clanging around others. We're trying to *attract* people, not repel them.

So how do we prepare for love? I've got some ideas on this, and the only supplies you'll need are a Bible, a journal, a pen, and an unassigned window of time.

. . .

I loved Lauren's chapter on prayer because there is perhaps no greater act of preparation than to begin your day in prayer. In fact, the best way to accomplish every preparatory act I'm going to suggest to you is to first ask *God* to accomplish it in you. When it comes to preparing to love others, a fantastic way to begin is by praying, "God, would you help me to love?"

Do you think God will honor that prayer? I know with certainty that he will. The apostle John wrote in 1 John 4:7-8 that we are to "continue to love one another, for love comes from God." He went on to say, "Anyone who loves is a child of God and knows God. But anyone who does not love does not know God, for God is love."

We simply can't love God, in other words, without loving people. And we can't love people apart from also loving God.

Back to what you can practically do, if you're hoping to prepare to love. Ask God to help you. That's step one. Next, make a daily practice of reading the Bible and writing down your prayers. I won't belabor what Lauren has already so adequately covered, but I will echo the importance of spending regular time with God. God is the one who gives us vision. God is the one who broadens perspective. God is the one who plants creative solutions to even life's toughest problems *right inside our minds*. Where else can we go to gain such wisdom? Make a practice of going to God. And as you read the Bible and find yourself pausing on a word or an idea, turn that word or idea into a prayer. Stop reading, and write that prayer down. Ask God to form in you the thing he says in his Word he will do.

Years ago, as our family continued to grow beyond what most people defined as normal, I had an epiphany. If I was going to successfully care for my wife and all these kids, I was going to have to tend to their myriad needs. Seems obvious, right? It should have been, I suppose, but the reason it wasn't obvious to me is that to meet their needs, I was going to have to *not* meet some of mine. I wasn't so sure I liked that prospect, so for quite some time, I kept prioritizing my wants, my needs.

Eventually, as a result of those early-morning Bible reading sessions with God when I was faithfully jotting down my prayers, I noticed that my prayers were sounding a little . . . selfish. It wasn't as overt as "God, could you please make these kids less needy?" but it was close. In my heart, what I wanted God to do was give me some space. Some relief. Some alone time. I wanted a moment of silence—can you relate to that? And all the while, I bet God in heaven was waiting for me to lay down my will and pick up his.

As a football coach, I always believed my primary role was simply helping players be the best they could be. In the same way, as a dad, I believe my primary role is to help my kids be the best they can be. The belief was there. Now I needed to back it up with action.

The epiphany was less a lightning-bolt moment and more a slow unfurling of a change I needed to make. I needed to become less selfish. I began by asking God.

I committed Philippians 2:3-4 to memory: "Don't be selfish; don't try to impress others. Be humble, thinking of others as better than yourselves. Don't look out only for your own interests, but take an interest in others, too."

The clarity of those verses was a punch in the gut. "Don't be selfish"—it doesn't get clearer than that. But once I caught my breath again, I was motivated to change. By the Spirit's power, I knew that as I asked God to transform this part of me, he would be faithful to see it through. I have no idea if my self-centered tendencies will ever fully be put to rest in this life, but I can tell you that I'm better than I used to be. I think Lauren would agree with that statement, anyway. *I'm better than I used to be.*

So come to God. Sit with God. See what God's Word has to say about the struggles you presently face. Pause as soon as you relate to something in Scripture, and turn those verses into a request of God. Before you know it, you'll become more loving as a person. You'll become less selfish. Or more generous. Or less combative. Or more patient. You might just be a *delight* to be around.

PREPARE TO LEARN

When I started at NBC, I knew next to nothing about sports-casting. Sure, I'd been around sportscasters for years and had consumed more than my fair share of their input before, during, and after every game I played or coached. But understanding a job and doing that job, I would discover, are two very different things. Another Coach Noll maxim I picked up along the way was his definition of pressure. "Pressure is what you feel when you don't know what to do," he would say, counsel I really took to heart. Months before the first game I analyzed on national television, I was keenly aware that I had no clue what to do once I sat down in that particular seat. Not wanting to feel pressure on that first night—or any night, for that matter—I decided I'd better seek out some answers to what I was supposed to do.

Being a coach at heart myself, I really appreciate solid

coaching. To sort out how to thrive in my new role, I went in search of input from people who could coach me on being a sportscaster—and on not fumbling on live TV. My learning curve was steep, but brilliant people such as Executive Producer Sam Flood and Senior Producer Bruce Cornblatt walked me up that curve one step at a time, offering me expertise on everything from where to look when the cameras were rolling to how to nail my pacing and more. "What else can you tell me?" I'd ask them. "How can I get better—fast?"

If I could sit across from you and talk about this topic, I'd start by asking what it is you're hoping to get good at these days. Are you in the same situation I was in all those years ago when I needed to learn how to thrive in a new job quickly? Are you a student working toward a new competency or a specific degree? Are you a teacher who needs to learn a subject more thoroughly before you can pass along that information to your students? Have you recently picked up a new hobby or sport? Are you determined to learn a new language? Do you want to write a book? Learn to cook? Something else?

Our son Jordan is determined to be a professional chef someday—is that you, too? Are you eager to improve your knife skills, master the quick pickle, or sort out the nuances of a specific cuisine?

Whatever it is for you, I'd advise you to do the same three things I did, both when I became a coach for the first time and when I became a broadcaster for the first time: find a couple of encouragers, ask them specific questions, and then listen carefully to the answers they give.

First, find your encouragers. These are people who have done or are doing the thing you hope to someday do. When you're looking for encouragers, be sure to seek out not only those who possess the expertise you need but also those who have a kind, caring demeanor. You need folks who will *guide* you, not goad you. I call them encouragers for a reason! For me, in this latest career move, Sam and Bruce were my guys. They cared deeply about my success and were willing to invest hours upon hours of conversation to help me see both what I had done well and what they believed I could do better next time.

Once you identify those encouragers, spend some time jotting down questions you'd like to ask them. You may not be able to tackle your entire list in the first meeting, but simply declaring to yourself the questions you'd like to ask will go a long way in steering the moments you do have together in a productive direction.

And finally, whenever you get time with your encouraging experts, be sure to listen well to every response they give. Come to those interactions with an open mind, an open heart, and open hands that are ready to receive. Don't defend yourself or make excuses whenever they mention a growth opportunity. Instead, smile, nod your head, and say, "Thank you for caring enough about me to tell me the truth. I am grateful for your feedback and commit to incorporating your input as I go forward."

Be respectful.

Be teachable.

Be a lifelong learner, and you'll go far.

. . .

A final thought on this idea of preparing to learn: if you can't seem to find a living, breathing expert on the thing you're hoping to learn, just grab your phone. There are many avenues for learning these days: podcasts, documentaries, websites, books, and more. In particular, books have been written on every conceivable subject, and by availing yourself of the condensed knowledge contained in a book, you'll leapfrog ahead in your understanding. When Lauren and I adopted our first child, I listened to lots of books on parenting a blended family. How was I supposed to know how to be a dad to a child I hadn't fathered, when I'd never done that before? Books told me how.

After our son Jamie died, I was given many books on grieving the loss of a child. How could I keep living when my beloved boy had died? Books showed me how.

Still today, when I'm feeling stagnant in any aspect of my life—spiritually, physically, mentally, emotionally, intellectually—I can turn to a book, absorb an author's hard-won advice, and be better for it every time. I've heard of people who are so serious about improving that they read an entire book each day. They must know how to speed-read, because to me that seems an utterly impossible task. But the motivation is one I understand. Books can serve as mentors to you and me. Leaders are readers, it is said. It's a sentiment I agree with and a fine segue to where we're headed next.

PREPARE TO LEAD

Prepare to love. Prepare to learn. And lastly, prepare to *lead*. When I consider the various spheres of influence in my life today, I come up with half a dozen or so key arenas. I am an influencer in my nuclear family and in my extended family. I am an influencer in Lauren's and my circle of friends. I'm an influencer in my hometown of Tampa, at our church, and in the men's Bible study I help lead with my buddy James Brown.

You might say I'm an influencer in my role as a broadcaster as well, since the words I speak are heard by so many people. Anyway, my point is that in any given week, I have the opportunity to influence lots and lots of people, just by showing up to the things I normally show up to. And the same is true for you.

You, too, have various spheres of influence, places where your mere presence changes the course of things. You are a daughter or son, for starters, intentionally placed in a family of origin. You probably know and perhaps spend time with at least some of your extended family members as well. You may be married. You may have children. You may live near neighbors or within the context of a broader community. You may work outside the home and therefore have colleagues, direct reports, a boss. You may produce books or other materials that reach hundreds, thousands, millions of people. You may be part of a church.

Regardless of the specific spheres of influence in your life, the question I have for you is this one: Are you stewarding them well?

Stewarding those relationships effectively means showing up prepared.

I think of Lauren's and my role as emergency foster-care parents. As Lauren mentioned earlier, those cries for help from the agencies trying to find families who will take in children—who by no fault of their own have landed in desperate situations— never, ever come in the middle of the afternoon, when we are awake, alert, and cruising through our day. No, those calls come at ten, eleven at night. So, years ago, we decided that one of the ways we could prepare to lead the kids who might be joining us unexpectedly was to have the house ready for them. We purchased two high chairs. We bought a toddler bed to slip into one of our other children's rooms and a fold-up bed to keep on hand. We rounded out our collection of brightly colored plates, utensils, and cups. Lauren constantly stocks the fridge and pantry with kid-friendly snacks. We had—and continue to have—intentional conversations about how to respond to a foster-care need in the middle of the night, so that when it happens, we're not only physically prepared but emotionally prepared as well. Stewarding our relationships with the children who come through our home means showing up prepared.

I think about my coaches' Bible study, which has always been a virtual gathering because of how many different locations we're all in. When it's my turn to lead the study, you'd better believe I put some thought into every word I plan to say. None of this "Hey, fellas, hope you don't mind if I just shoot from the hip today. . . ."

No, I care too much about those friends to show up unprepared. And so I study. I pray. I work out the questions I want to ask. I log the hours so our gathering can be as fruitful as possible.

Or what about my primary broadcasting partners, Mike and Drew? Because there is an endless amount of information a person could consume prior to game night, it's legitimately impossible for me to come 100 percent prepared. Same goes for them. But because of how deeply we respect each other and the slots we fill, each of us knows that the other two are going to show up ready to roll. We'll never be as ready as we wish we could be—that much is true. Yet when we all put the time in to get as close as we can to that desired state, we honor those we're seeking to influence for good—in this case, our bosses, our colleagues, and you, the viewing audience.

Now I want to ask you: Who resides inside your spheres

of influence? Are you taking the necessary steps to be able to influence them for good?

. . .

The Bible includes a proverb about a guy who refuses to prepare for winter during the warm summertime months. The writer referred to him as "lazybones." "How long will you sleep?" he asked. "When will you wake up? A little extra sleep, a little more slumber, a little folding of the hands to rest—then poverty will pounce on you like a bandit; scarcity will attack you like an armed robber" (Proverbs 6:6-11). I can tell you from firsthand experience that you won't be able to love well or learn well or lead well until you *prepare diligently* to do so. You leave that preparation to chance and go through life winging it, and you'll never have the type of influence that honors God or the people he has for you to serve. *Poverty* and *scarcity* will indeed characterize our lives, both in terms of how we experience them now and in terms of the legacy we one day will leave.

But the opposite is also true. In his counsel to first-century slaves who were made to submit to earthly masters, the apostle Paul told them to "work willingly at whatever you do, as though you were working for the Lord rather than for people" (Colossians 3:23). He assured them that good would come to them when they viewed their work this way: "Remember that the Lord will give you an inheritance as your reward, and that the Master you are serving is Christ" (v. 24). Even though you and I aren't slaves serving masters here on earth, we can approach our work this way too. We can come prepared. We can work hard. We can honor both God and our team.

5

PERFECT ENOUGH

Choose to Move

Lauren

As you can tell, preparation is *critically* important to my husband. Yet he would be the first to tell you that during his coaching career, at some point his staff and players had to quit preparing and start playing, or else they'd miss the game they were so busily preparing for. I'm all for being prepared—I'm a huge fan of having all my ducks in a row, in fact—but let's be sure to quickly acknowledge that the time always comes when you've got to quit prepping and start *performing*, because the big event you've been anticipating happens to be underway already.

At the end of Luke 10, we read the well-known story of Mary and Martha, sisters to the famed Lazarus, whom Jesus raised from the dead. Jesus had been ministering throughout the countryside and now was headed with his disciples to Jerusalem, when they "came to a certain village where a woman named Martha welcomed him into her home," verse 38 reads.

> Her sister, Mary, sat at the Lord's feet, listening to what he taught. But Martha was distracted by the big dinner she was preparing. She came to Jesus and said, "Lord, doesn't it seem unfair to you that my sister just sits here while I do all the work? Tell her to come and help me."
>
> But the Lord said to her, "My dear Martha, you are worried and upset over all these details! There is only one thing worth being concerned about. Mary has discovered it, and it will not be taken away from her."
>
> LUKE 10:39-42

I liken Martha's posture to that of a guy like Peyton Manning hunkered down in the team's locker room going over his pages and pages of notes as game-day kickoff is happening out on the field. "Peyton, Peyton," I can just hear Tony saying, "you're so consumed with the details that you're *completely missing the game*."

Ludicrous, right? And yet far too often, well-meaning people like you and me and countless others need to quit *anticipating* every once in a while, and get out there and *act*. We spend our time fixing and fussing and fretting while Jesus sits there, shaking his head. *I'm here*, he whispers, time and again. *You can quit your prep work now.*

Sometimes Jesus shows up as a neighbor in need. Sometimes it's a colleague who has the need. Or a child, which is the version that really tugs on Tony's and my hearts. And when we stop prepping and start tending to those in need—really and truly tending to them—we do what Jesus said in Matthew 25:40, which is that as we serve "one of the least of these" we in fact are serving him.

. . .

During the COVID-19 shutdown in the spring of 2020, several friends and I decided that we needed to do something about the fact that because the local schools were closed, many students weren't getting a nutritious breakfast or lunch. Many people from my generation would think only of the educational ramifications of school shutdowns, but these days, too many students rely on schools for their meals as well. In the Tampa area, around 150 schools are qualified as Title 1 schools, which means that at least 40 percent of the students hail from low-income families. Those students receive free or reduced-price breakfast and lunch each day, so when the pandemic rolled through and closed their schools' doors, which also closed their schools' *lunchrooms*, they were in dire straits. Remember that principal telling Tony and me about his faculty's "Friday afternoon sweeps"? The issue isn't unique to that school.

Once enough of us moms realized these kids right in our own city didn't have enough food to eat—or enough proper food, anyway—we banded together. We solicited donations of breakfast bars and bagels and sandwiches and chips and fruit and juice boxes and more. Then we put the word out to families of one school in particular that if they had hungry kids, they could come to the school at nine o'clock each morning to receive food for the day.

In my mind's eye, it would work like a drive-thru, where parents would pull up, volunteers would load food into their vehicles, and off they'd go. It didn't exactly work like that. For starters, we needed to check in each family by finding them in a computer database to be sure they had a student enrolled in the school. It took forever to accomplish that seemingly straight-forward task, which caused a backup of massive proportions. And did I mention that some kids had just ridden over on their bikes? Trying to figure out a way to balance all the boxes of food in their baskets required engineering acumen none of us possessed.

The entire situation prompted moms who were sitting in those backed-up vehicles to jump out of the driver's seat, head over to where our volunteers were frantically trying to serve the ever-increasing line of hungry families, and pitch in. They grabbed stacks of the little activity kits we'd prepared for the kids to do at home, raced back to their cars to hand the kits to their kids so they'd have something to do while their moms selflessly served, and rushed back over to us to ask, "What can I do? Where can I be most helpful? How can I lighten your load?"

I stood there smiling from ear to ear. It was messy. It was imperfect. But within minutes, we'd found gloves and masks for all those extra volunteers, and the line was eventually dislodged.

We went through this same routine for weeks, and those nights after passing out meals all day, I'd put my head on my pillow and think about how grateful I was that hundreds of kids weren't going to bed hungry that night, and that in addition to those kids' physical needs being met, some of their emotional needs had been met too.

. . .

Not long after that season of serving, Tony and I received the late-night call about Dontae and Kallie. It had been a wildly busy day, as most of our days are. It was our bedtime, and we were exhausted. Our plates were already so full with obligations and family plans that had been on the calendar forever and decisions waiting to be made that the very real temptation before us was simply not to answer the phone. Had we let the call go to voice mail, this caseworker just would have called the next family on the list.

Let me tell you why I picked up.

As we've mentioned already, because Tony and I are registered as an emergency foster-care family, there is a certain obligation that accompanies answering these middle-of-the-night calls. But I didn't answer out of obligation that night. I answered out of love.

As I crossed the room to grab my phone, all I could think about was the fact that sitting right next to the person calling was a child—or in this case, more than one child—who was hurting and scared and worried and feeling very alone. I didn't know what had happened yet, but I knew it was something bad. Kids don't end up with Child Protective Services in the middle of the night unless something very bad has gone down. I thought about how if I didn't answer that call, another family would be called. And another after that. Given the late hour, if *everybody* chose to let the call go to voice mail, those kids would have to sleep in the caseworker's office, huddled together in a sterile environment, having no clue why they were there and what had happened to the adults who took care of them. You'd have picked up too.

. . .

Candidly, I would much prefer to receive opportunities to serve in the middle of the day when I'm rested and wearing something other than running tights and have my hair and makeup fixed. I'd rather God ask me to step in and help when my living room is organized and all the bathrooms are clean and I've had time to prepare a little snack for whomever is coming over and make accommodations if we're talking about overnight guests. But guess how often this idyllic scene has unfolded for me? Exactly never. That's just not how life works. It has been said if you want something done, give it to the busiest person you know. I'm one of those busiest people, and do you want to know what is true of every busiest person you know? We're too busy to clean the house! It's not that we don't *love* a clean house; it's just that when the options are a spotless home or a service opportunity seized, we're going to go for impact every time.

I couldn't agree more with my husband about the importance of preparation. I myself take great pride in being ready for the day as best I can. To stop by the Dungy household on a school night is to see a whole lot of scurrying around. As the kids are getting ready for bed, they know they are to put out the next day's school uniform; load their backpacks and place them by the door to the garage; make their lunches and have them ready to pack; and fill their water bottles before pushing them into the little side pockets on their backpacks. We do this so mornings can unfold without sheer chaos ensuing. I've seen what a lack of preparation does to our mornings, and rather than enjoying a peaceful send-off as the kids leave for school, it's more like a downward spiral into anxiety and rage.

The pandemic has only tightened our processes here. This year, the kids' schools alerted us parents to a rule change on their part. No longer would parents be allowed to drop by the school midmorning to deliver something a student had accidentally left at home. If a child forgot his lunch, for example, the school would provide a voucher for a meal that day, which would be charged to the parents' account. If a child forgot her homework assignment, she'd have to make arrangements with her teacher to bring it the next day. But no more frantic text messages sent from school hallways that read, "Mom! You've got to come by the school!!"

With as many kids as we have, we leave as little as possible to chance. So this rule change? I say bring it on. It only reinforces our preparedness bent.

But in the very next breath, I will say this: if you are foregoing opportunities to pitch in and help someone who is obviously in need because your delusions of grandeur have you hurrying and hustling in hopes of being *just a little more prepared*, you've simply got to emerge from fantasyland, step into the fray, and *act* on that person's behalf. To insist on being like Martha, who was so busy making preparations for Jesus that she missed being with Jesus, is to squander the resources God has entrusted to you. It's to essentially hoard those things for yourself. It's treating your life as a reservoir, despite God's call on all believers' lives to flow like a river—coursing, active, giving, serving, bubbling over with refreshment and life.

So go ahead and make preparations for the serving you may someday do. Just be sure that when the game starts, you're out there on the field—making plays, getting dirty, being alive. Now let's talk about how to get that done.

IF YOU'RE ABLE TO SERVE, THEN SERVE

One day during Jesus' earthly ministry, as the Gospel writer Luke reported, an expert in religious law asked Jesus this question: "Teacher, what should I do to inherit eternal life?" Jesus answered, "What does the law of Moses say? How do you read it?" (Luke 10:25-26).

The expert in the Law quoted from Deuteronomy: "You must love the LORD your God with all your heart, all your soul, all your strength, and all your mind." And "Love your neighbor as yourself" (v. 27).

"Right!" Jesus replied. "Do this and you will live!" (v. 28).

The man was trying to test Jesus, so it should come as no surprise that he challenged the answer Jesus gave. "And who is my neighbor?" he asked (v. 29), which is when Jesus told a tale.

The Parable of the Good Samaritan, as this story is known, is the tale of a Jewish man who's attacked and left for dead by bandits. A priest happens by but does not help. A Temple assistant strolls by but also does not help. At last, a man from Samaria, a despised region in those days, sees the Jewish man, feels compassion for him, and actually stops to help. He bandages the man's wounds. He gives the man a ride into town and covers a hotel stay and anything else he may need. He even plans to check on the man when he returns from his travels, to be sure he has fared okay.

After sharing this story, Jesus looked at the expert in the Law and said, "Now which of these three would you say was a neighbor to the man who was attacked by bandits?"

The man answered, "The one who showed him mercy" (vv. 36-37).

"Yes," Jesus replied in the next verse, "now go and do the same."

Again, the man's question—"Who is my neighbor?"—was meant to challenge Jesus in the heat of the moment. It was sort of like he was saying, "Oh, *yeah*?"

But I find that when posed from a pure heart, "Who is my neighbor?" is actually a fantastic question to ask.

If you are wondering where to start on this grand serving adventure . . . if you're ready to take action and are curious how to begin . . . then consider coming to God in prayer with that earnest question on your lips. "Father," you might pray, "who is my neighbor today? Who has a need that I might help meet? Where would you have me point my energy and time?"

I prayed this prayer countless times during the shutdown of 2020 and was astounded by how many times the Lord instantaneously put a specific person or couple or family on my heart and asked me to provide for a specific need. Often it involved picking up extra food, usually from the barbecue restaurant where our son Jordan works—if those bacon-studded collard greens can't fix it, it can't be fixed—and dropping it by at the dinner hour. Only later would I learn just how important those meals had been for the families who'd received them—delivered, according to them, "at just the perfect time."

Isn't that just like God?

On the move at the perfect time.

. . .

Whenever we're in Eugene, Oregon, our favorite vacation destination, our young son Jalen loves to visit the local skate park. Over time, he began noticing that whenever we went there, several people who seemed to be homeless were hanging out there too. He started asking Tony and me questions: Why were the men living in a park? Didn't they have a home? Were they hungry or thirsty? Did they have any friends?

One day, as we were preparing to head to the park, I saw Jalen stuffing his backpack with as many water bottles as the bag would hold. "Jalen," I said, "why do you need all that water? We'll only be gone for a few hours."

"It's not for me, Mom," he said.

We arrived, and before the van had come to a complete stop, out popped Jalen, backpack unzipped, hand reaching for those bottles. He marched straight for the men who had set up something of a campsite on the edge of the park and started passing them out. "Would you like some water?" he said with a huge smile. "Here! Take one! I brought them for you!"

I had the opportunity to meet a new friend's ten-year-old daughter recently, and we were talking about how Jalen is forever giving out water bottles and how lately he'd progressed to also passing out food. "His heart is really geared toward people who are down on their luck," I said, "people who just need a fighting chance to get back on their feet again."

My friend said that her daughter, Prisca, is similarly wired. She told me that one afternoon she found Prisca organizing all sorts of goodies into little piles.

"I got them on Amazon," Prisca told her mom. "Is that okay?"

She'd assembled gallon-sized Ziploc bags containing travel toothbrushes and tubes of toothpaste, mini bottles of water, individually packaged hand wipes, hand warmers, granola bars, and men's athletic socks. Then she'd dipped into the family's cash drawer in the kitchen and stuffed five-dollar bills into each bag before loading the packages into both her mom's and her dad's cars. "Keep one bag under your driver's seat at all times," she instructed them, "so that whenever we come across someone standing on a street corner who is hungry and thirsty and sad, we have something to put into their hands."

Amazing insight for a child to realize that we are called to care for people as Jesus would.

. . .

I have dear friends who are just *so good* at listening to other people's concerns. Their "neighbor" is often the person whose heart is breaking and who simply needs someone to talk to.

I have friends who have the spiritual gift of generosity. Their "neighbor" is often someone who is up against a financial wall they cannot scale.

I have friends who seem to have supernatural radar for moms who are having a rough day. Their "neighbor" is often the mother utterly dripping with kids who is mortified in line at Target as she waits to check out because her toddler is melting down. "Here," those friends are known to say. "You go right ahead and cut in front of me. I insist. And can I hold that precious baby for you while you do?"

The point is, you may not see all the needs in the world, but it's likely you catch a few. Think about this question: *Which ones do you catch?*

Do you have a soft spot in your heart for people who are ostracized and friendless?

Or for those whose basic food and shelter needs never seem to be met?

Or for single moms working dawn to dusk to keep life afloat for their families?

Or for people battling addiction who are desperate for a way out of their pain?

Take your God-given inclinations to the foot of the cross each day and ask God how to see what he longs for you to see. He might point you toward someone whose need is one you're accustomed to meeting, or he might broaden your horizons and point you toward a person you'd never otherwise see. Either way, I think you'll find that there is nothing quite like the adventure of being divinely directed each day.

IF YOU'RE UNABLE TO SERVE, THEN SUPPORT

A huge motivator for my orientation toward service is the Word of God. I have spent decades meditating on Scripture, and for any serious reader of the Bible, you just can't get away from the call to serve. Let me point you to a couple of passages I find most compelling. In Acts 20, Luke recorded these words from the apostle Paul: "You know that these hands of mine have worked to supply my own needs and even the needs of those who were with me. And I have been a constant example of how you can help those in need by working hard. You should remember the words of the Lord Jesus: 'It is more blessed to give than to receive'" (vv. 34-35).

In Matthew 5, Jesus told his followers, "You are the light of the world—like a city on a hilltop that cannot be hidden. No one lights a lamp and then puts it under a basket. Instead, a lamp is placed on a stand, where it gives light to everyone in the house. In the same way, let your good deeds shine out for all to see, so that everyone will praise your heavenly Father" (vv. 14-16).

Here are two more:

The book of Hebrews reminds us, "God is not unjust. He will not forget how hard you have worked for him and how you have shown your love to him by caring for other believers, as you still do. Our great desire is that you will keep on loving others as long as life lasts, in order to make certain that what you hope for will come true" (6:10-11).

Paul, writing to the church at Galatia, said, "You have been called to live in freedom, my brothers and sisters. But don't use your freedom to satisfy your sinful nature. Instead, use your freedom to serve one another in love. For the whole law can be summed up in this one command: 'Love your neighbor as yourself'" (Galatians 5:13-14).

There are many more verses we could point to, but I won't bombard you with them here. Plus, they'd all be reinforcing the very same point: if we are "in Christ," then we are "in service" to those around us. We are to be Christ's hands and feet to a world that is desperately in need.

I bring all this up because I want to remind us of the expectation God has for us once we are knit to his heart through Christ. He is activating a redemptive plan throughout the earth, and when you and I sign up to serve the needs we see around us, we are by definition serving that supernatural plan.

But this is also true: there are times in life when the best you can do is keep your own situation, your own family, afloat. Life has a funny way of throwing curveballs, and you know as well as I do that on occasion there is simply no good way we can show up for others because we're barely able to show up for ourselves.

I am thinking here about the year that Tony and I lost our son to suicide. And also the year that Tony was fired from the team he adored. And the year that has just passed, as I watched my dear mom die. I could recount two dozen suffocating seasons, and the fact is, so could you. We all have seasons of surplus, and we all have struggles, too. The important thing to remember is that God promises to use them both.

. . .

In the previous section, we talked about the joys of serving when you have something important to give. Those are great times, aren't they? On days when we are filled up with God's empowerment and our circumstances feel manageable and our relationships seem healthy and our kids are doing as they're told, it is an absolute *gift* to be able to serve other people. It's a *delight* to help meet a need.

And yet those days don't come around all the time. We often experience a whole 'nother kind of day.

There's the day when your special-needs kid can't get the help she needs. There's the day when your sister calls you to say Mom isn't doing so well. There's the day when your husband reports that he's been delayed on his business trip another day or two. There's the day when your phone doesn't stop ringing . . . more needs, more needs, more needs. There's the day when you feel like a cold is coming on, like your head might just explode.

There's the day when your teen confesses she slept with her boyfriend last night. There's the day when your boss explains to you that you're not needed at the firm anymore. There's the day when you bury a lifelong friend—stage IV cancer, so dire, so fast. There's the day when your project just fizzles . . . so much time and effort lost.

On any given day, a thousand things could happen that rip the rug from under your feet. Yet I'm here to tell you *even on that day*, serve.

Tony and I were talking recently about whether it's easier to serve God out of our surplus or out of our struggle. Since we've known both situations in life on countless occasions, we had plenty of fodder for each view. At first blush, it seems like serving God from a place of surplus would be the far easier course. I mean, for those who have a six-figure income, what's a hundred bucks to someone in need?

But the conversation was more nuanced than that. Because while it *should* be easier to serve from surplus, most times it's in the struggle that we're drawn close to God. And when we're nearer to the heart of our heavenly Father, we're nearer to serving gladly in his name.

So here is what I want to say about the seasons of struggle you and I often find ourselves in: don't forsake service during those seasons. Instead, *support those who are serving well.*

. . .

I've always loved the passage from Exodus 17 about the nation of Israel defeating the warring Amalekites. Just after the Amalekites ambushed the Hebrew people, the great leader Moses commanded his protégé, Joshua, to "choose some men to go out and fight the army of Amalek for us. Tomorrow, I will stand at the top of the hill, holding the staff of God in my hand" (vv. 8-9).

Joshua did as he was told and fought Amalek's army. "Meanwhile," the passage continues,

Moses, Aaron, and Hur climbed to the top of a
nearby hill. As long as Moses held up the staff in his
hand, the Israelites had the advantage. But whenever
he dropped his hand, the Amalekites gained the
advantage. Moses' arms soon became so tired he
could no longer hold them up. So Aaron and Hur
found a stone for him to sit on. Then they stood
on each side of Moses, holding up his hands. So his
hands held steady until sunset. As a result, Joshua
overwhelmed the army of Amalek in battle.

vv. 10-13

The image of those two men holding up the arms of Moses
is one I love to ponder. When we face seasons of struggle, we
may not have it in us to show up on the front lines of the battle.
Even so, what a gift it is to someone who *is* fighting there to
have us support them from either side.

If you are walking through a particularly challenging season,
this message is for you. Go look for a Moses who is hip-deep
in the real-deal battle and ask, "How can I support you in your
good work?"

Do you know a couple serving as foster parents? Consider
asking them if you can watch their kids for an afternoon or
evening while they catch a few one-on-one hours.

Do you know someone having major health issues? You
might ask if you can clean their kitchen or run errands for
them one afternoon.

Do you have a friend who recently suffered a serious loss?
Maybe a coffee date would encourage their heart . . . just the
two of you and some uninterrupted time.

Does your church collect food or clothing for people in need? While you may not be in a place to facilitate that hand-off directly, could you arrange to bring a few things to church next week in support of that worthwhile cause?

Might you pray more intentionally for your neighbor who faithfully shows up to tutor urban schoolkids each week?

Might you slip a grocery-store gift card and a thank-you note to the mom of your kid's soccer pal who is constantly funding team snacks?

Might you speak an encouraging word to your colleague who spends his weekends building homes for people fighting their way up from poverty?

I can tell you from firsthand experience that even when you're walking through the darkest of valleys, coming alongside someone who's serving will lift your spirits every time. It's okay to lean on their belief when your own faith is faltering. It's okay to contribute secondhand. It's okay to give yourself a break when you need one. It's okay to take the supporting role.

And then, whenever you're ready, that front line will be waiting for you.

DON'T FORGET TO FIGHT THE LIES

Whether you are prompted to serve or prompted to support the servant, let me leave you with two lies that you will have to continuously fight if you hope to help others over the long haul. The first one is this: "I'll serve once I get my life under control."

One day a few weeks ago, I had a good idea of how things were going to unfold. I needed to take the kids to school and get to my Bible study, but after those two obligations were out of the way, I was resolved to spend some unhurried time with a friend whose adult daughter was in crisis mode.

I can't even tell you what happened, but before I knew it, my day got hijacked by two unexpected errands, a traffic jam that ran clean through the center of town, a lengthy and ultimately futile text chain with my child who'd forgotten both his lunch and the school's rule that disallowed me from bringing it to him, and a sick baby who got sent home from day care because nobody is interested in being around a fussy, feverish kid.

The temptation on days such as that one is to come away thinking, *See? My life is just too crazy right now. I have no business trying to help.*

It's an understandable tack to take, right? I myself have taken it several times. But here's the problem with caving to the lie that you can't show up for someone else until your world is perfectly under control: *you miss the magnificence of God.* In the same way that the Israelites must have felt like giving up when they came to the seemingly impassable Red Sea, you and I look at the craziness, the busyness of life, and assume there is no way for us to help. But just *look* at how God showed up for them. Might he show up for you and me too?

There is a big difference between being in a season of real personal struggle and dealing with the general craziness of life. Everyone is busy. Everyone is occupied. Everyone has obligations. Everyone has plans go awry. Don't make the mistake of assuming that one derailed day renders you unfit to serve the purposes of God. Instead, exhale your frustrations, laugh at how absurd life can be sometimes, and ask God to show you how he will use the failed plan for his good.

When your heart's desire is to glorify God by caring for the people he sent his Son to save, he will part seas you had no clue he was capable of parting. He will give you back the time you missed out on. He will restore the connection you feared was lost. He will bring peace to your harried insides. He will honor that desire every time.

. . .

"I'll serve once I get my life under control": that's the first lie we're tempted to believe. The second one is this: "I'll serve once I get *myself* under control."

I've spent the last twenty years advocating on behalf of children in need, specifically those who need a forever family and long for a forever home. Children are an important group to serve because they are among the most vulnerable people in the world. They need food and water, shelter and clothing, companionship and love, and unless someone helps them with those things, they simply will not receive them on a daily basis. Children live at the mercy of us adults. When they are young, anyway, they cannot choose where they live, where they attend school, or where they go to church—if they go to church at all. They cannot dictate the density of their physical nutrition, the quality of their family's emotional health, or the pace of their own spiritual development. Those things are all decided for them, and children carry the results of those decisions with them for a long time—in some cases, for a lifetime.

It follows, then, that when a caregiver of a child—a parent or grandparent, an auntie or uncle, a boyfriend or girlfriend, a family friend—is unwilling or unable to properly care for that child, a whole lot of chaos ensues. Because that child is so incredibly vulnerable, so deeply reliant on the adults in his or her life, it is utterly devastating when those adults don't show up. Children need us to show up spiritually. They need us to show up emotionally. They need us to show up physically. When we don't, their world falls apart.

Now, I want to discuss this idea of showing up for the simple reason that when people realize how high the stakes are for a child who is not receiving the care and consideration she deserves, they tend to shy away from serving that child. I've seen it happen thousands of times. They see the child. They see the child's great need. They have resources that could help meet that need. But they do nothing to get involved.

Maybe they're sitting in a church service and hear a talk about children in the developing world who don't have food to eat. They could sponsor one of those children and ensure that a child gets fed, but they don't. The need just seems too great.

Or maybe they learn on the evening news that a local adoption agency is hosting an event that weekend to find forever homes for the final hundred children in the county who haven't yet been adopted. They see the need and could actually help with that need but don't. The need just seems too great.

It could be that right there in their own family a child has a need that is going unmet. They see the need and could absolutely help! They could bring a meal over once a week. They could give the child a ride to church on Sundays. They could make themselves available for the hour on weekdays between when the child gets home from school and when the single mom gets home from work. Whatever it is, they could actually be of assistance, and yet they just can't get themselves to jump in. Something in them taunts them with the question *Who do you think you are, to try to help a child?*

The situation feels too unpredictable.

The stakes feel too high.

The need just seems too great.

They feel inadequate or ill-prepared.

They wonder if they really have what it takes.

They believe some specialization or expertise exists in those who are better suited for the job.

They think they're too young.

They think they're too old. (I should mention here that on the day of my mom's death, she still had an adoptive son living in her home who was *seventy years* her junior. The woman practiced what she preached, fostering and adopting children even after she was well beyond retirement age.)

They think they're too rich.

They think they're too poor.

They think they're too introverted, or too extroverted, or too exhausted by "playing with kids."

In short, they assume that if they decide to try, they'll fail for sure.

If I may pass along one piece of encouragement on this subject, I would tell you to remember that it takes so very little to have a big impact in the life of a child. When caregivers don't show up for the children they're supposed to be caring for, those kids are set up to fail over time. In the same way, though, when caregivers *do* show up, those kids are set up to thrive. Each time Tony and I have taken in children in emergency foster-care situations, I've been amazed by how elated those kids are over the simplest acts of kindness and attention. They don't need grand, over-the-top gestures. They don't need wild displays of emotion. They don't require fancy accommodations.

They simply need us to show up. They need an adult whose face shines with the presence of God to greet them by name, welcome them in, offer them a warm hug, provide them a little snack, show them the place where they can rest, pray with them in a calm voice, and remind them that they're safe, that everything is going to be okay.

If you've been wondering if you have what it takes to serve the needs of a child, consider starting small. Support someone who is serving a child already, as we talked about before. Get around foster families. Get around people who have adopted children. Befriend someone who heads up to the local elementary school and reads to children once a week.

Then start praying for God to give you opportunities to see the needs in your community that *you* might help meet.

The stakes really are high when it comes to children in need. But every bit as true is this: you plus God's empowerment and presence equals enough, every time.

. . .

Listen, only our good Lord in heaven knows precisely how he will use your life for great impact in the days and years to come. Same is true of mine. My singular hope for us both is that *we won't get in his way*. It's a real tragedy when a person wastes her one precious life on selfishness and greed. But equally devastating is when you or I spend it preparing for a game we never play. God asks us to fight the good fight and run with endurance the race he has set for us (see 2 Timothy 4:7 and Hebrews 12:1). This is undeniably action-oriented language. These and other verses ask us a significant question: Are we acting on God's prompting?

May we act on God's prompting today.

6

"WE" OVER "I"

Choose Team

Tony

Four or five weeks into the NFL season last year, I was asked during the broadcast for my thoughts on a news story that had surfaced involving a head coach not flying home with his team after a road game. The team had lost the game, its nineteenth straight loss, actually—a streak dating back to the previous season. The team was miserable. The coach was miserable. Everyone probably needed some space. This was the rationale the coach gave a few days later, anyway, but something still didn't square for me. *You don't abandon your team,* I kept thinking. If that coach had personal commitments in the city where his team had played that road game, then he could have flown home with his team, made sure everyone was settled, and taken the very same plane back to the city he'd just left. Inconvenient, maybe. But a far better option than the one he chose. When you're part of a team, you have a responsibility to everyone on that team—to show up, to stay invested, to care.

I was eleven years old when I first understood what it meant to be part of a team. Richard Holmes was my peewee football coach, and that team bus never went anywhere without Coach Holmes at the helm. Granted, the rest of us were kids, and it would have been dangerous and even illegal for us to go off unattended by an adult in charge. But Coach Holmes didn't stick around because of legalities. He stuck around because he was part of the team. He was in it with us guys whether we won or lost, whether he felt great or was sick, whether he had more important things going on in his life or not. (Given the stakes, of course there were always more important things, but never once did my teammates and I pick up on this fact.)

What these two anecdotes have in common is the theme of *self*. A teammate who is habitually selfish will soon find himself without a team. But a teammate who is habitually *selfless* will garner his team's respect for years—even decades—to come.

THE IMPORTANCE OF SELFLESSNESS

A few years ago, I released a book on teamwork called *The Soul of a Team*, a modern-day parable about a fictitious NFL expansion team that had to learn how to thrive. More than any other topic I'm asked to speak on at various gatherings, people want to hear me talk about teamwork. They want to know how to get people who are diverse in every conceivable way to come together, to work together, and to win. That's the magic question: How can we all pull in the same direction, when we're so accustomed to going our own way? The book was my attempt at answering that question. The four letters in the word *soul* framed my response: if a team's going to operate as a team, it's going to be because of *selflessness, ownership, unity,* and the sense that there's a *larger purpose* at work. In this chapter, I'd like to offer up the rationale for why those four tenets are so critical to the life of a team, as well as explain why the order of the four matters greatly, and how one tenet leads to the next.

For starters, the reason I was so irritated by that NFL coach neglecting to fly home with his guys following the road loss was that, as I saw it, the first principle of teamwork had been violated. The choice was a selfish move.

. . .

If you were to look up the *Merriam-Webster's* definition of the word *selfless,* you'd find that it means "having no concern for self; unselfish."[1] Keep reading in that entry, and you'll see a list of synonyms, my favorite of which is the word *considerate.* To consider something is to think carefully about it. It's to gaze upon something, to absorb it. It's to take something or someone into account.[2] Human beings have no trouble reacting to life in a selfish manner. We come into this world selfish, as you've probably noticed if you've ever raised a child. By instinct, we know how to fight for our perceived rights, we know how to get what we think we deserve, and we know how to defend things once we get them. What isn't so natural is *considering* others' needs, *gazing upon* others' realities, and *taking into account* others' desires. So while there is a vocal contingency these days standing against the concept of selflessness on the basis of not wanting people to "lose themselves" in the process, I remain steadfast in my belief that there's something to this selflessness thing. I've seen too much good come from it to believe otherwise—both for the person doing the considering and for those being taken into account.

As with all the big choices I make about how to live life, the roots of my interest in living selflessly are found in Scripture. In Philippians 2:3-4, the apostle Paul reminds us that if we want to go God's way in life, we'll need to lay down our natural tendencies and pick up some supernatural ones. He says, "Do nothing out of selfish ambition or vain conceit. Rather, in humility value others above yourselves, not looking to your own interests but each of you to the interests of the others" (NIV).

I don't know what you think when you read those words, but the phrase that comes to my mind is *high bar*. Not doing "some things" out of selfish ambition seems a more reasonable ask. Doing *nothing* out of selfish ambition feels like an unattainable goal. And yet I will say this: the more you and I approach life as a team sport instead of a solo endeavor, the easier selflessness becomes.

Let me see if I can explain how this works by laying out a first-century scene. As the story goes, a religious leader came up to Jesus one day and asked, "What should I do to inherit eternal life?"

Jesus looked at the man and said, "You know the commandments" (Luke 18:20) and then went on to summarize a few of them: don't commit adultery, don't murder, don't steal, and so forth. To which the man said, "I've obeyed all these commandments since I was young" (v. 21).

It was this man's way of saying, "Yeah, yeah, yeah. I've got all that down. What else do you have for me?"

Jesus had something in mind. "There is still one thing you

haven't done," he said in verse 22. "Sell all your possessions and give the money to the poor, and you will have treasure in heaven. Then come, follow me."

The next verse is classic understatement: "But when the man heard this he became very sad, for he was very rich" (v. 23).

You and I would have been sad too. Give up *everything* and offer the proceeds to the poor? High bar, if ever there were one. In the next breath, Jesus spoke these iconic words to the crowd gathered that day: "How hard it is for the rich to enter the Kingdom of God! In fact, it is easier for a camel to go through the eye of a needle than for a rich person to enter the Kingdom of God" (vv. 24-25).

What Jesus was asking that man to do went way beyond a financial transaction. He was asking him to see the poor as teammates, as people *not to be overlooked*. Remember, Jesus didn't ask everyone to sell all their possessions and give the money to the poor as a prerequisite to following him. What he *did* do was ask people to let go of the things that were keeping them from caring about other people, serving other people, taking care of other people, and loving other people well. If money was in the way, let go of money. If power was in the way, let go of power. If prejudice was in the way, let go of prejudice. Whatever was keeping people from *valuing others above themselves*, as that verse in Philippians says, had to go. This is what teamwork's about.

I delivered this message to the Indianapolis Colts by reading this passage during the first team meeting of our Super Bowl year and said, "We talk a lot about the importance of our shared value of teamwork, but how deep does that value run?"

I reminded our guys that, at some point during the year, one of the coaches was going to ask each one of them to do something that probably felt as impossible to execute as the rich ruler selling all his possessions and giving the money to the poor. "Are you going to hold fast to the value of teamwork then?" I asked them. "Are you going to go all in?"

If we had enough men say yes to those questions along the way, I told them, then we stood a chance at having a big year. The biggest year. I made eye contact with many of those players as I ended my speech and then asked, "Will you be one of those men?"

. . .

One of the men in the room that day was wide receiver Reggie Wayne. I didn't have to ask the question of him because I already knew what he'd say. He'd already *proven* what he'd say. I've written about this situation before, but it bears repeating that during the last game of the Colts' 2004 season, it was Reggie Wayne who left $150,000 on the table when he put the team's needs above selfish gain. Entering the final weekend of the season, we'd already locked in our playoff positioning. It wouldn't matter in the standings whether we won or lost the game, so I made the decision to rest many of the starters, knowing that the playoffs were coming the following week.

What I didn't know was that Reggie had a performance clause in his contract that season stating that eighty receptions would trigger a $150,000 bonus. He had seventy-seven catches when I pulled him out of the game. Reggie never said a word. No bad body language. No outward signs of disappointment.

On the plane ride home, one of the other players pulled me aside and informed me that three more catches would have been a real difference-maker for Reggie. As you'd expect, I felt terrible. But when I approached Reggie later to apologize, my mood brightened. The guy was *teamwork* through and through. "Don't worry about it, Coach," he said with a grin. "You did what was best for the team, and that's what matters!"

Reggie might have been the one who had missed out on $150,000, but I think I felt worse about the loss than he did.

It's worth noting that the next week, in the first game of the playoffs, Reggie Wayne set team records for most catches and most yards in a playoff game. And that Reggie Wayne went on to catch *far* more than eighty balls per season for the next six years.

He understood that team victories demanded teamwork. Selfish interests had to be put aside.

I hope I emulate this sort of spirit in my own life. I think back to my early days coaching in the NFL and how much I used to love to play nine holes of golf on Friday afternoons with another member of the Steelers staff. I was never very good, but I really enjoyed those outings. Lauren and I didn't have any kids at the time, and she worked all day on Fridays, so I wasn't needed at home. But once the children arrived and I was part of a team—and that team needed me at home—my thinking needed to change. The golf outings had to stop.

Same goes for fishing. Once Lauren and I moved to Tampa, nothing delighted me more—recreationally, anyway—than inshore Gulf fishing for redfish, those eight- to ten-pound deep-sea rockfish that are so prevalent around here. For years, I'd take my boys fishing with me, and those times made for some great memories. But once they were old enough to declare for themselves how they wanted to spend their free time, fishing didn't make the cut. A typical fishing trip takes about six hours, door to door, and quickly it became apparent to me that if I wanted to hang out with my kids, I was going to have to start loving what they loved to do. Which is why these days you are more likely to find me hanging out at a local skate park than doing just about anything else. So be it. If it's good for the team, it's good for me—that's the way I view things now.

When a team is underperforming, the first question to ask is this: Has each of the team's members truly caught the spirit of what selflessness demands? There's no use moving ahead until the answer there is *yes*.

THE OWNER'S MENTALITY

The second tenet of teamwork is *ownership*—which to me means faithfulness to owning one's role.

Let's talk for a minute about washing dishes. If you're doing the math, then it may have occurred to you that given how many people live in our house, a big part of our lives centers on meals. Planning for meals. Shopping for food for those meals. Preparing meals. Eating meals. And nobody's favorite, cleaning up after meals. I don't remember when we finally figured out a system for maintaining sanity amid all the meal-related activities, but I do remember that it was Lauren who cracked the code. She looked at me one day and said, "Tony, I don't care if you ever buy me a better car or fancy jewelry or if you ever take me on amazing trips. All I want is a second dishwasher. You get me that, and you never have to get me anything else."

Knowing a good deal when I see one, I said yes. And I must admit, the addition just made things *work*. No longer did we deal with a sink full of dirty—or clean, for that matter—dishes. No longer were all the dishes dirty at the same time. No longer were we forever waiting on the dishwasher to cycle through. Brilliant.

Our strategy goes like this: the youngest child in the household who isn't an infant is given the official job of Clean Utensil Put-Away-er. For a long time, that person was Jaela, but then when Dontae and Kallie came to live with us, Dontae took over as utensil head, and Jaela got promoted to cups. All the way up the ranks, each Dungy has a job: this person moves plates and bowls from the clean dishwasher to the cabinet; that person clears the table; this person rinses used dishes; that person loads rinsed dishes into the dirty dishwasher; and so forth. What this means is that immediately following a family meal, 100 percent of us get up, head to the kitchen, and get busy doing our assigned work. (You'd think that because we keep adding children to the mix, eventually I'd get released from kitchen duty altogether, but somehow Lauren keeps finding ways for me to assist.) In a matter of minutes and in the spirit of many hands making light work, the cleanup effort is complete, and nobody is overly worn out.

I bring all this up because it's a perfect picture of ownership, of teammates owning their respective *roles*. When you're in our home, you're a Dungy, and as such there's a role for you to play. This goes for dinner guests. It goes for relatives who are in town. And it goes for our kids' friends, who sometimes eat with us. And to the extent that everyone is willing to shoulder his or her specific responsibility, chaos is kept at bay, order is maintained, and Mrs. Dungy is one happy woman. Actually, Lauren has put thoughtful systems in place for all sorts of things in addition to kitchen cleanup, and as I said, when everyone is willing to own his or her role, things just *work*.

But the opposite is also true: if someone refuses to pitch in and help, the whole deal falls apart.

A team can only be effective if team members own their roles—whether they *like* those roles or not.

As you'd expect, examples of this (both positive and negative) abound in the world of sports. Players who are serious about excelling in their specialty are a lot more fun to coach—and a lot more effective—than those who aren't. Fortunately, most of the men I coached over the years were big-time owners of the roles they played. When you looked at them, you saw their role; the two identities were that intertwined. They thought carefully about what they were doing, both on and off the field, knowing that the team was counting on them to cover their role. Yes, they owned their roles by showing up on time and ready to go, and by playing hard every single day. But their ownership went beyond that to include things that affected how high they could soar.

They also owned their *development*. The best teammates are ravenous learners. They're the ones who study how they performed so that they can do it better next time. They study how other people play their role so they can incorporate those best practices too.

They owned their *drawbacks*. Nobody is good at everything. Great teammates are honest with their team about what they can't yet do well so others can jump in and pick up the slack while they shore up whatever is lacking. I should mention here that sometimes a drawback is ongoing, such as when a teammate has a physical, mental, or emotional obstacle that simply can't be overcome. Our son Jordan deals with some physical limitations that, barring divine intervention, will be with him for the rest of his life. His friends know what he can and can't do, and they make room for him each time they hang out.

On the other hand, sometimes a drawback is momentary, and with a little assistance can be easily addressed. An entertaining example of this comes to mind. During one of my first years in Tampa, a player I coached came up to me and told me that his dog had gotten loose. We were right in the middle of practice, and I had no idea what he was talking about.

"Coach," he explained, "my neighbor called and told me my dog somehow got out, and now he's running around the neighborhood, and nobody can get him back home."

You hear it all as a head coach, but this one was new even for me.

I shook my head and grinned. All I could think about were the forty-six other guys on the field that day who needed *this* guy to perform, to cover his role. But then I looked into this player's eyes and saw a hint of terror there. I knew what he was thinking. He was thinking about how much he loved his dog. He was predicting how his dog was going to keep darting here and there and eventually get run over by a car. In his mind, he was already saying goodbye to his pet, which meant he wasn't focused on our practice at all.

"Go take care of your dog," I said as I cuffed his shoulder. "Get back here as soon as you can."

In the end, we wound up getting far more production out of that player by covering for his absence than we ever could have hoped to get by demanding that he stay. Yes, we need to take care of our responsibilities to the team. But drawbacks will sometimes occur. When you've been faithful nine out of ten times to perform the role your team needs you to play, on that tenth occasion when you need some assistance, teammates will line up to help you out.

Let me give you a final type of ownership I saw in the best players I coached: they always owned their *mistakes*. I'm known as a pretty even-keeled type of person, which is probably why players I've coached along the way get so excited when I amp up and lose my cool. It doesn't happen often, which only adds to its allure. In all honesty, I can think of only two times throughout my four decades in the league when I said something I knew I'd regret. Okay, maybe three. In any case, after each of those infractions, once the moment had passed and I had a chance to regain my composure, I made sure I went to the people who'd been impacted and apologized for what I'd said.

The same was always true for many people I worked with on various teams. Nobody expected them to be perfect, and they weren't. What made them special, though, was their willingness to own the things they got wrong.

"That was my responsibility, and I botched it."

"I fell asleep on the job, and I'm sorry."

"I really got that wrong."

"My mistake."

"My fault."

"My bad."

These are things I heard those people say with great regularity. There was no finger-pointing, no passing the buck, no shifting blame. Just ownership, ownership, ownership—all day, every day. They owned their roles. They owned their development. They owned their drawbacks. They owned their mistakes. All mission-critical components, considering where we're headed next.

ON (NOT) FIGHTING FOR UNITY

The third tenet of teamwork is *unity*, and here's what I've noticed about this subject along the way: when the first two tenets are present and ordered correctly, this third one takes care of itself. If you have off-the-charts ownership from the players on your team, but those players are selfish, only caring about their own roles, then you will never achieve a spirit of unity. You may have a standout individual contributor or two, but you won't be successful over time as a team. Similarly, if you have a bunch of selfless teammates who neglect to really own their roles—not to mention develop and excel in those roles—then you'll be about as effective on the field as an empathetic surgeon who just can't make the incision because of the pain he imagines his patient to be in.

But when you have teammates who are *first* selfless and then are faithful to playing their roles *in service to the good of the team*, you've got a team worth playing for. You've struck gold, from what I've seen.

I remember seeing both sides of this dynamic play out during my first two years with the Steelers. That first year, training camp was rough. The team had experienced success in the form of two Super Bowl victories, and now was the time to cash in. Guys were refusing to report to camp while their agents negotiated contracts until late in the summer, and the net effect was sheer turmoil. The concept of "teamwork" took a back seat. Selflessness was nowhere to be found—at least among some of the higher-profile guys. And ownership? Well, it was tough to own what hadn't formally been offered to you.

I didn't realize how awful it had been until my second year with the team. Starting on day one that year, I saw incredibly talented guys sacrifice all sorts of individual opportunities and accomplishments so that the overall team could win. Time and again, I saw a level of ownership that left me shaking my head in disbelief. My teammates were in it to win it—to a person, this was true. "You'd better start making arrangements to come to the Super Bowl," I remember telling my mom about two weeks into training camp that season. "Whatever winners have, we've got it. There's something special about this team."

That something special is unity. It's everyone marching toward the same goal. It's *selfless ownership* from every teammate. It's people being where they're supposed to be, doing what they're supposed to do—not just anecdotally but all the time.

There is a lot of talk these days about our society needing unity. For obvious reasons, most of which have been endlessly detailed in the news, I agree with the sentiment. What I might take issue with is how we ought to go about achieving the unity we say we desire. Not to minimize the problem, but in my view, whenever unity is lacking, one of two things is to blame: either someone somewhere is being selfish, or someone somewhere is neglecting his or her role. In this way of thinking, unity isn't so much something we pursue as it's the natural by-product of other, wise pursuits. As you know, I believe those pursuits are selflessness and ownership. When they're tended to, unity flows.

Peyton Manning approached his role as QB of the Colts with a high degree of selflessness and a high degree of ownership. Because of this, he was compelled to drive six hours round trip during the off-season to help rookie receiver Anthony Gonzalez learn his role. Anthony wouldn't complete his studies at Ohio State until June, and Peyton knew that waiting until

June to practice with Anthony would be cutting things too close to training camp. So he took it upon himself to climb into his truck and head three hours east to Columbus once or twice each week to work out with our new guy.

Eleven-year NFL veteran running back Edgerrin James approached his role in the same manner: high selflessness, high ownership. Partway through the 2001–2002 season, Edgerrin tore his ACL, which is the absolute toughest injury for someone in his position to return from. A big part of the anterior cruciate ligament's job is to hold the femur and tibia in place during deceleration, which is a big part of any running back's game; once it's torn, players often have trouble cutting as fast as they used to cut. We were told that it would be nine months before Edgerrin could hope to heal from surgery, but within six months, he was playing flag football with his friends. His commitment to his team led him to work out like a maniac, in the end shaving months off his recovery time and more quickly getting him back on the field.

That's unity having its way, that sense that we're in this thing together and are prepared to fight for the other's good.

Closer to home these days, whenever I spot my son Jordan voluntarily making the little kids' lunches in the morning or whenever I hear a sibling who is able to drive offering his brother or sister a ride to wherever that younger child wants to go, I think, *That's what unity looks like.* It's "hospitality . . . without grumbling," as one Bible verse says (1 Peter 4:9, NIV). Nobody asks my older kids to do these things. But because they approach their roles selflessly and with a high degree of ownership, they are naturally moved to go beyond what's expected, simply for the good of the team.

I guess what I'm saying is that we don't have to fight for unity. We just have to choose selfless ownership, and unity will start fighting for us.

. . .

In 1981, after I'd been hired onto Coach Noll's coaching staff, I went into his office one day and said, "Coach, what's my job?"

I knew my title: I was the Steelers' defensive assistant. What I wasn't so sure about was what that title meant. What, exactly, did a defensive assistant do? Of course I understood that I was to support our defensive coordinator in his efforts to craft game plans and prepare for each week's opponent, but in terms of the actual practical steps I was to take, I was pretty much in the dark.

In classic Chuck Noll fashion, which from where I stood equated to simple, straightforward, effective communication, Coach said, "Your job is to help your players play better."

Elegant, right? I loved that about his style.

Thankfully, though, he went on: "You've got to get to know each of your players. You've got to figure out what things they need in order to improve. And then you've got to find a way to get them those things."

At the time, I had seven guys I was responsible for. And from that conversation forward, I made it my mission to know those men inside and out—to know what made them tick, what motivated them, what discouraged them, what approach made it easier for them to learn. I'd go into my office after practice and jot down notes of the observations I'd made that day. And while the effort demanded great sacrifice sometimes, the rewards were greater still. Each time one of my players blossomed in some undeniable way, I felt sure the satisfaction welling up in me would come spewing out.

Years later, when I was a team's head coach, I'd apply the same principles as Coach Noll. To each of my staff members, I'd say, "Your job is to help your players play better."

They'd eye me a little suspiciously. *That's it? That's all you have to say?* To which I'd talk about selfless ownership, about seeing their men's needs and making it their mission to help meet them. But at the core, what I was after was unity, and I was clear on how unity would be achieved.

I took things so far as to start hiring for unity. As a job candidate interviews for higher and higher roles in the NFL, head coaches and GMs and owners generally want to talk with him or her about offensive or defensive philosophy, about *strategy*, about X's and O's. All I wanted to know was how this person was going to take fifty-plus men from disparate backgrounds and educational experiences who were different ages, who were different races, who held different political views, and who wanted *wildly* different music in the weight room and get them to work as a cohesive unit. Oh, and did I mention that while I was open to a variety of coaching styles, I expected to hear only positive comments from our staff?

Less yelling.

Less cursing.

Zero demeaning.

"Thinning the herd," anyone?

Eventually the scouts who helped us secure staff for open coaching positions got a grasp on the type of coaches I wanted. Eventually they understood that I wasn't just interested in stellar individual contributors; I wanted *teammates* to join our team.

And before you accuse me of shooting myself in the foot with my unusual hiring filter, be reminded that along the way this strategy landed me assistants with names you might recognize: Jim Caldwell, Leslie Frazier, Herm Edwards, Rod Marinelli, Lovie Smith, and Mike Tomlin. Unity for the win.

Throughout those years, I began to view my role as husband and father through the same lens. I'd devote myself to seeing— really seeing—Lauren's needs and then making it my mission to help meet them. Still today, I'm always on the lookout for ways large and small that I can lighten her load and help her to thrive and enjoy her days. Less than an hour ago, for example, when I was on the phone doing an interview in advance of this book's release, Lauren popped into my office with her new water bottle in hand and a look on her face that said, *Help?*

Lauren and some of her running friends have been trying for months to kick their Coke habit, and one of them suggested that they all buy these giant water bottles that you fill up in the morning and carry with you all day long. On the side of the bottle, there are little tick marks labeled *8:00 a.m.*, *10:00 a.m.*, *Noon*, and so forth to *8:00 p.m.* The idea is that you drink eight ounces of water every couple of hours and are fully hydrated by day's end. Maybe replacing soda with water would help, the thought went. Lauren was immediately in.

Just now, Lauren was trying to get out the door and wanted to take her water bottle along, but she hadn't paid close enough attention to how all the parts fit together when she dismantled it to wash it before its first use, and now she was stuck. She needed to get to an appointment. She wanted to take her water bottle. And she couldn't get the pieces to fit. Which is why her expression was saying, *Help?*

Without even thinking about it, I waited for the interviewer to pause and then said, "Excuse me, but I need to tend to something on this end for just a moment." And then I turned and helped my wife.

Now, I'm all for appropriate boundaries in relationships. And had I assessed the situation and realized that helping Lauren was going to take an inordinate amount of time, I might have muted myself on the call and asked her if I should reschedule my meeting or if we could sort things out after my call.

But given the situation, I knew that in about twenty seconds' time, I could have the water bottle reassembled and could send my wife into her day with a smile. I want to be a selfless husband, just as she is a selfless wife to me. I want to own my role as her spouse, the one person in the world who is always for her and who is always willing to help. And because of those two aspirations, her problem is my problem too. Unity works like that.

On the fatherhood front, the same dynamic is in play. Listen, when you foster as many children as Lauren and I have fostered, every last selfish whim gets dissolved. There isn't *time* for selfish whims. When we started this foster-care journey, I should have had a T-shirt made that read, "Who has a need? How can I help meet it?" As it relates to my family, that's all I've cared about for years. And if there has ever been any doubt about whether it really is "more blessed to give than to receive," as Jesus is quoted as saying in Acts 20:35, I'm here to tell you, *those words are true.*

This hints at the fourth and final tenet of teamwork, the *L* in the *soul* acronym. It stands for *larger purpose*, you may recall. If you'll stick with Lauren and me for a few more chapters, we'll reach a full treatment of that tenet in chapter 10.

TEAM WINS ARE THE BEST WINS

Several years ago on NBC Sports, I interviewed star receiver Julio Jones, who now plays for the Tennessee Titans. During that conversation, he told me that he grew up loving football, even as he also played basketball and ran track. I learned that Julio became the high school state champ two years in a row, in both the long jump and the triple jump, and the state champ for the high jump during the 2007 indoor season. I asked him why he hadn't pursued track and field in college. He'd been named the 2006–2007 Gatorade Track and Field Athlete of the Year for the state of Alabama. Division I schools would have clamored to have him run for them.

His answer made me grin. "I never liked track," he said. "I'd win the 100-meter," he continued, "and I'd feel great about that accomplishment, but there was no one to celebrate with. So I'd celebrate by myself. Compare that with scoring a touchdown, when a whole *team* would be freaking out. I loved that someone had to throw the ball, and that a bunch of guys had to protect that throw, and that someone had to catch that ball—it took all of us, working together. *That* win is way more fun."

I thought, *This guy understands teamwork.* He had individual talent that he could have used only for himself, but he chose to invest it in a team. Biased though I may be, a team win *is* always more fun. It's true in football, and it's true in life. Things are more fun, more interesting, and far more rewarding when you need me, and I need you.

7

PICK YOUR BATTLES

Choose Steadiness

Lauren

It's a little ironic that I'm the one writing the chapter on steadiness, because between Tony and me, he's the far steadier person. Yet maybe it's okay that I'm here with you talking about this subject. Sometimes working from a place of vulnerability allows a person to convey truth more powerfully than speaking from a place of victory can.

As I write these words, the calendar tells me we're mere days away from a new year. It's wonderful to have something new, isn't it? A blank page, a clean slate, a fresh start. I'm part of the group that still uses a paper planner, and something about seeing an entire year laid out in front of me, ready to be stuffed with hopes and dreams and plans, lights me up every time. The things we'll do! The places we'll go! The connections we'll make! I am a high-energy person with big ideas, and it remains one of my life's greatest joys, this practice of plotting the future, day by day.

And yet I'm also old enough to have learned a tough lesson, which is that life almost never goes according to plan. Oh, sure, there are exceptions. About a month ago, I woke before my alarm. I nudged Tony, and together we prayed for the day ahead. I made a cup of hot tea and had a bite of breakfast, double-checking my plans for the morning, the afternoon. I tugged on running tights, filled my water bottle, and out the door I went. By the time I logged on to a conference call I was due to participate in at ten o'clock, I'd already enjoyed time with Tony, checked the kids' bags and lunches for school, cleaned out my car, tended to a half-dozen administrative to-dos, completed a 5K with my run group, showered, dressed, put on makeup (thank you very much), and made a second cup of tea.

Following that call, it was smooth sailing even after the kids arrived home from school. I'd prepared a snack for them, dinner was taken care of, and I was able to sit and chat with the older kids, who always have situational knots that need untangling.

I'd planned my day, and then I'd worked my plan. Things had gone just so, and I was elated, I have to say.

It's worth noting that the reason I remember that day so specifically is that days like that one are a rare occurrence for me. I'm guessing they're a rare occurrence for you as well. Most of the time, it feels like life takes in our thoughtful, carefully crafted plans, balls them into paper wads, and throws them across the room. Someone tracks mud into the kitchen on the very day you mopped the floor. Someone forgets something at home, and now you're tasked with delivering it. Someone runs out of gas, and you're made to kiss your morning's agenda good-bye. Actually, that last one happened to Jordan just a few weeks ago. He's twenty-one years old. He's an experienced driver. He's considered our family's most reliable driver, in fact. And yet still I got the call. "Uh, Mom? I think I'm out of gas. . . ."

He'd picked up a few of his buddies and headed over to a local grill called Bahama Breeze to grab some lunch, but when he climbed back into his truck to head home, his truck wouldn't start. This is not an old truck, I should clarify. It's a new truck that Jordan bought with his own hard-earned money. And guess what new trucks have? They have sensors that tell a person when he's getting low on gas. All sorts of bells start chiming and lights start flashing and icons start telling you, "Refuel. Refuel. Refuel." But did Jordan see any of these signs? He did not. And so there he sat in the Bahama Breeze parking lot with his friends until his loving parents could come help him out. Clearly, "Rescue twenty-one-year-old son, who will run out of gas at 1:00 p.m." wasn't on my calendar for that day. But there it was, life disrupting my plans yet again.

Weightier still, looking back at the past year, I didn't include plans for Jordan to have surgery during what Tony and I thought would be a routine checkup with his doctor in Palm Beach. A thirty-minute appointment turned into an unexpected over-night stay right before our eyes.

I certainly didn't include plans for my husband to be hos-pitalized while we were on vacation in Oregon. He recovered beautifully, but boy, what a ride that was.

Nor did I include plans to say goodbye to my wise, winsome mother, Bird. I rejoice that she is in heaven now, but still—what a terrible loss that has been.

Most recently, I didn't have plans to foster children who had been so horribly abused. Even now, after receiving so many little girls and boys with open arms over the years, I remain emotionally unprepared for the horrors children sometimes face.

I wonder, what annoyances or challenges or devastations did you face last year that you certainly did not plan for? What interruptions distracted you from what you thought you'd be doing? What eagerly awaited plans got thwarted? What losses did you sustain? Especially in today's world, life feels less knowable and controllable than ever. We're learning to hold loosely to every commitment we make: Will it happen? Won't it happen? Who's to say?

At any given time in the Dungy household, ten to fifteen bodies are moving about—more if any of the kids have friends over. I tell people that *controlled chaos* is about the best I can ever hope for, even as I cling tightly to the dozens of systems I've established over time to help things run as smoothly as possible. But what this means is that on any day, as the person who manages most of the day-to-day activities for our family, my plans can be uprooted in a dozen or more ways. Early on in our foster-care experience, I saw the writing on the wall. Despite my thorough planning, it was utterly impossible to foresee the fact that one child was going to have a scheduled court visit with his biological mom on the very day that another child was supposed to perform in a school play, which was the same day that Tony needed me to attend a function with him. And this would happen not just anecdotally but seemingly *all the time*.

I'm guessing you're nodding your head in recognition about now. Do you relate to the deep desire to clone yourself on some days, so that everything that needs to get done can get done? Especially for my friends who are single parents, this not-enough-of-me-to-go-around dynamic plays out a million times each day. I know there are books that promise to help us carve out sanity amid life's maddening pace, but who has time to read them? There's always something else to do.

Even considering these realities—that we're under constant pressure to get everything done, that despite our careful planning life tends to do what it wants, that the very people we love most can be the biggest disruptors of our day-to-day world—you might think I'd be an absolute pro at taking things in stride because I've lived this thing called life for quite some time now. You might think that given how long Tony and I have had upward of a dozen little people in our forever care, I'd have figured out how to respond to these realities in a way that is measured and mature. You might think I'd be an endless fount of wisdom when it comes to calming the inevitable chaos that erupts when things don't go our way.

I won't say you'd be wrong, exactly. But wrong-*ish*—it's probably that.

Yet as I mentioned before, I *am* learning. I'm growing. I'm better than I used to be. And what I can tell you is life works better from a steady state. When I paused to think about how I've gotten better about taking things in stride, I realized that, as syrupy as it may sound, Tony has unknowingly been my guide. He truly is the steadiest person I know. There are a lot of moving pieces in our lives—especially in his, because of his responsibilities with NBC. When there are this many variables, the opportunity for things to shift or go wrong is sky-high. Yet regardless of the problems life presents him with, Tony stays strong. When plans change, he nods. He ponders. He silently thinks through a work-around.

When people don't do what they said they would do, he exhales his frustration and pivots to a different solution.

When someone offends him or makes unkind statements about him, he refuses to strike back. I can recall multiple occasions during Tony's coaching career when a sportswriter would unfairly criticize Tony in the newspaper and then request an in-person interview with Tony the next day. I was always amazed by Tony's graciousness in giving time to someone who had just lambasted him the previous day. "Sure," he'd say. "I've got five minutes. What would you like to talk about?"

When one of the children does something he or she shouldn't have done, Tony remains kind and calm as he gathers information about what happened. He prays for wisdom and guidance as he's piecing together the situation. And together with the young offender, he sorts out a go-forward plan.

Now, this all represents the *ideal* state, you understand. I'm not saying my husband is superhuman, but he does possess the rare ability to practice this pattern most of the time. I'd be hard-pressed to find exceptions, which is why he's my role model for steadiness. But even the wobbliest people alive should take heart because there is a path forward. I've studied what Tony does, and the steps he chooses to take when life lets him down are steps *any* mere mortal can take.

THE TELL

Those who know me will laugh when they see me using a gambling analogy because I'm not exactly a gambler. Have never played a hand of poker in my life, in fact. But a word from that world so perfectly describes what I'm after here that I had to use it. The word is *tell*.

In card games, a player's "tell" says to the other players at the table, *This is what I'm going to do.* Maybe the player's tell is leaning back in his chair, or putting chips on the table with a little extra force, or glancing at the competition when she usually keeps her gaze fixed on her cards. It doesn't have to be a big, sweeping gesture—most tells aren't. But if you're paying attention, you'll notice some slight change in behavior that tips you off about how the person is really feeling.

On the emotional front, in my experience, everyone has a tell—a small shift in behavior that tells those nearby that the person is about to lose control. Actually, for some time I believed that I, for one, had no tell. But then I asked my kids for their perspectives on the matter. When giving their opinion on adults' behavior, unfortunately, children never lie.

It turns out my tell is the phrase, "What were you thinking?"

Technically, it's a question, even if a rhetorical one. The children informed me that they've come to learn that whenever I ask that question, I'm not really seeking a response.

A friend told me her husband's tell is wrapping his right hand around the steering wheel one finger at a time. "He'll start with his pinky finger and slowly grip the wheel digit by digit without saying a single word."

That same friend admitted that when she is about to lose it at home, she goes upstairs and starts furiously folding laundry. "If you're folding clothes at some random time," her daughter once told her, "I keep clear of the room."

I've heard of other tells along the way: a prolonged, meaningful sigh; the biting of one's upper lip; inexplicably leaving the room; sitting on one's hands; a slow, back-and-forth shaking of the head; falling silent in a conversation; tapping one finger on a surface; smiling at an inappropriate time; rubbing the forehead; a cold, dead stare.

Even my beloved Tony has a tell. When he's frustrated or disappointed, he shakes his head and mutters, "You have got to be kidding me."

When he's *really* frustrated or disappointed, he says, "You have *got* to be kidding me."

The kids and I hear that latter version emerge from Daddy's lips, and we go on high alert: *Uh-oh. Things must be really, really bad.*

Out of curiosity, what's your tell? When things don't go as planned or some grand disruption shows up in your day, what's the reflexive thing you say or do that signals your compromised emotional state?

Do you roll your eyes?

Do you click your tongue?

Do you fidget with your fingernails?

Do you purse your lips?

Do you do a five-second inhale?

Do you mutter some version of "You have got to be kidding me"?

If you think you don't have a tell, think again. Ask a loved one what yours is and then get back to me. *Everyone* has a tell.

We all have tells, and our tells are reflexive—that's the big idea I want to establish in your mind. I don't *mean* to look at the child who has run out of gas and say, "What were you thinking?"

Tony doesn't *mean* to put his head in his heads and say, "You have got to be kidding me" when our preschool-age son intentionally breaks our other preschool-age son's favorite toy truck.

My friend doesn't *mean* to obsess over her family's laundry in the middle of a busy workday.

Our tells just happen. They happen without our input. They happen without our guidance. Much of the time, they happen without even our *awareness*. They are the automatic ways we acknowledge that life has somehow let us down. But while these subtle reflexes may seem inconsequential, they play a vital role in our ability to grow in steadiness. Just as they tip off others about our emotional state, they can tip us off too. Once we hear or see ourselves delivering our tried-and-true tell, we can choose carefully what happens next.

THE TEMPTATION

Once you know your tell, you'll start to see what you naturally do next. Left to our human-nature responses, we will escalate an already-frustrating situation by behaving in a manner that is thoughtless, selfish, and aggressive. One way this plays out in our home with greater frequency than I prefer is that, in an effort to take the dinnertime load off my shoulders some nights, Tony will offer to stop by the drive-thru at McDonald's and bring home food for the kids. Knowing my husband as I do, as soon as he makes that generous offer, I text him the order, line by line. We have a lot of mouths to feed, and the minds that go with those mouths have *ideas* about how they want their food prepared. No ketchup. Extra cheese. No lettuce. Extra onions. Large fries. Shake instead of a drink. On and on it goes. So I send all of this information to Tony and then stand there in the kitchen exhaling meaningfully. *I hope he gets this right.*

Twenty minutes later, Tony appears, paper sacks of food in hand. The kids start distributing everything, and that's when the grumbling begins. "Hey! Where's my large fries?" "This isn't right!" "I said *no* ketchup!" "There aren't enough burgers here!"

All heads swivel toward Tony.

"What were you *thinking*?" I say.

Now, let me push pause on this scene for a moment. While that rhetorical question may have slid right through my lips without my permission, what happens next is mine to choose. If I'm not careful, I will let my frustration take the win. I will add to the problem by saying, "I texted you every last detail, Tony. You *never* read my texts carefully. You have to *check the order* before you pull away from the restaurant. You have to *make sure* they got things right."

Any guesses as to how effective this strategy is in furthering the goals of harmony in our home and showing respect to my husband and modeling appropriate behavior to our kids?

Not effective, I think you'd agree.

Regardless of the precise steps I think should be taken in fast-food drive-thru situations, what has happened is what has happened. The question is *How will I respond?*

• • •

Ask any child psychologist around—or any parent, for that matter—and they will affirm the fact that we all are born selfish. You don't have to teach a child to say, "Mine." And while it would be nice if we progressed from this posture in the same way we progress from needing diapers or bottled milk, regrettably there is an innate entitlement to the human experience that can stick with us at every stage. Despite our physical growth, we can stay emotionally stunted. Even as full-grown adults, we can still think the world owes us certain things. We can still believe we deserve certain things. We can approach life with the notion that we are somehow *above* disappointments and setbacks. This thought, this belief, this approach shows up on the heels of our tell.

For people who struggle with steadiness—and I still count myself among them from time to time—the tell isn't the problem. The problem is that they don't use their tell as an opportunity to alter what happens next. So the tell surfaces, and instead of thinking, *Ah. I'm about to lose my cool here,* they just keep running on autopilot. And in case you haven't noticed, human nature's autopilot makes for a bumpy ride.

This is how an errant "What were you thinking?" shifts into an outright verbal attack regarding how my husband "never gets it right."

It's how a meaningful sigh turns into an entire evening spent icing the other person out.

It's how a bitten upper lip morphs into standing up, storming out of the room, and slamming the door.

It's how fidgeting with fingernails becomes a fist put right through a wall.

All the blaming, shaming, and stomping around that happen in response to something not going the way we think it should happen right here, after the tell, every time we fail to wisely choose our next step. If we keep operating this way, we let a passing incident become a trend—and then a lifestyle. We become people who overreact.

Left unaddressed on a long-term basis, a sense of bitterness can take root. "Poisonous" is how bitterness is described in the

Bible (Hebrews 12:15). I can attest to the truth of this—I have a loved one who's been poisoned by bitterness for years. Nothing is *ever* this person's fault. No one can *ever* meet this person's high standards. Life *never* works out just right. Something's always, *always* wrong.

With this person, the tell always leads to huffing and puffing and blowing the house down. Pounding the table. Stomping the feet. Screaming. Face turning red. Fuming for days on end. Any time I'm around this person, I see myself with no holds barred. I see what I could become if I don't take steadiness seriously each and every day. I see the result of running way too long on autopilot, of being a person who simply refuses to take the wheel.

Thankfully, there's a better way.

We can choose a different way.

THE TURNING POINT

As I've been on this journey toward Tony-like steadiness, two verses of Scripture keep coming to mind. The first is from Romans 7, where the apostle Paul talks about how frustrating it is to be human. "I don't really understand myself," he writes, "for I want to do what is right, but I don't do it. Instead, I do what I hate" (v. 15). He goes on to say that it is his "sinful nature" (v. 18) that drives this maddening behavior, something that's true for you and me as well. What this means is that even though you and I don't necessarily want to erupt every time life—or another human being—disappoints us, if we let our sinful nature dictate our actions, we're likely to erupt every time. We're likely to take things further than they need to go. We're likely to veer toward the shouting, or the storming out, or the fuming-for-days thing some people are prone to do.

The second verse that comes to mind, also from the apostle Paul, sounds much more hopeful to me: "The temptations in your life are no different from what others experience," he wrote in 1 Corinthians 10:13. "And God is faithful. He will not allow the temptation to be more than you can stand. When you are tempted, he will show you a way out so that you can endure."

When we are tempted, God will show us a way out so that we can endure—what a useful promise this is. And as far as I have seen, even when the stakes are ridiculously high, three simple choices help us find that way out, that turning point we so desperately need. I'll show you how they played out in a recent situation I faced and then work through them with you one at a time.

. . .

I've shared with you that what made last year feel unbearable to me was losing my mom. She'd been diagnosed with a brain tumor, and it was like the residual effects of the treatments she had to endure and the secondary issues that cropped up once the tumor seemed to be under control conspired to take her down. She could never catch a break, which was devastating to watch.

As I mentioned, Tony, the kids, and I were on vacation in Oregon when things first started spiraling downward for my mom, and a real temptation for me on my eventual eastbound flight to Pittsburgh was to follow the unspoken but deeply felt *What are you* thinking, *life?* with a little entitlement parade. After all, my mom was one of the wisest, kindest, most beautiful women the world has ever known. She was godly. She was generous. She was gentle. She was fun. Like me, she loved to *eat*, and the conversations we shared over delicious meals could fill volumes upon volumes of books.

I adored her.

Everyone who knew her adored her.

And this was the thanks she got?

I was so disappointed. Not with God directly, although I'm sure that's how it seemed. Mostly, I was disappointed with life. With the nebulous way things were turning out.

I felt let down. I felt frustrated. I felt sad. But as I said, I hadn't given myself over to these feelings just yet. In fact, by the time that plane landed, I had adjusted my state of mind. By God's Spirit, my mind had been renewed. I reminded myself that I didn't have to rant and vent and fume; I could choose a different way. I decided that regardless of what was about to unfold in Bird's—and, by extension, my—life, I would receive reality with graciousness. I would treasure each minute I was given with my mom. I would keep praising God for his goodness, despite not knowing what was to come. And by God's power, that's exactly what I did.

Bird and I headed to each of her radiation appointments together, and while both of us were scared and increasingly tired, we loaned each other strength. During the bits of time between doctors and nurses popping in for various reasons, we'd plot our lunchtime locale. We'd fantasize about how good that hoagie or grilled-chicken salad or deli pizza was going to taste as soon as we left the medical center and then giggle over our expert distraction technique. We'd stop by the pharmacy on our way home to pick up the meds she needed, and during those car rides she'd ask about Tony and each of the kids as though she didn't have a care in the world.

I look back on those months I spent with Bird, and all I feel is gratitude. I'm grateful I wasn't so angry and outraged that I missed the moments altogether. I'm grateful she chose to set aside talk of the diagnosis, the prognosis, and the agonizing treatments from time to time to connect with me, friend to friend. I'm grateful for the graciousness and patience she exhibited at every turn—what a perfect role model she was for me.

I miss that woman dearly. She was one of the good ones.

Still today, as I'm confronted with setbacks and disappointments that are admittedly far less weighty than what Bird had to deal with last year, I think about how she approached the obstacles she faced. I think about how consistently she accepted what was, instead of demanding to get her way. That's the first of the three choices I mentioned before, choices that help us claim God's promise to always provide us a way of escape when we are tempted to do something unwise. It's to *receive reality as it arrives.*

Receive Reality as It Arrives

There's nothing like being emergency foster-care parents to remind you that life doesn't always work the way it should. The children with whom we've crossed paths are always in crisis, and crisis situations never reflect the best of humankind. There is addiction. There is abuse. There is neglect. There is hardship. And once children are taken from their parents, the parents have the added burden of trying to get them back. It makes for a difficult situation on every side—the parents' side, the foster parents' side, and the side of the social workers who are stuck in between. One of the reasons I'm so motivated to become an expert in steadiness is so that I can better minister to the kids we take in—and, by extension, to their moms and dads.

So, yes, while I value things like perfection and excellence and efficiency and orderliness and thoughtful systems, I also value a periodic reality check, which reminds me that things won't always be as they should be.

Talk to God

The second choice that helps us take God's promised way of escape from the temptation of losing our cool is choosing quite simply to *talk to God.* You might be surprised how quickly you can whisper a prayer to your heavenly Father—for wisdom, for insight, for peace. Let me give you three straightforward questions that I find God just *loves* to answer when I'm stuck between my tell and the very real temptation to erupt:

WHAT'S GOING ON HERE?

I realize this question doesn't sound like a prayer, but it is. Sometimes our emotions are so triggered by someone or something that we can't see clearly what's really going on. We're in a frenzy of feelings, and it seems that with every passing second, we spiral more and more out of control. Asking God for divine insight to see the truth of the matter helps us discern a mountain from a molehill. It helps us know how to frame our response.

When Tony and I parented our first three children, we often reacted to things that didn't necessarily warrant a reaction. We were perhaps overly concerned with their hairstyles, for example, and with their choice of outfits day after day. We had high expectations for how they appeared and behaved, which may have communicated something we didn't really mean. As we began parenting the next group of children, we realized that by choosing not to engage in battles over outward things, our corrections regarding inward things—issues of character and godliness and love—were more easily received and honored. That simple shift, one of the dozens I could cite, came from praying through disappointments instead of plowing through them in our own strength.

The next time you feel your blood pressure rising because things aren't working out the way you planned, pause and silently ask God, *What's going on here? Why am I so upset by this?*

Then wait for a hint of guidance. Your spouse may need a hug more than a public shaming. Your child may need a smile more than a rebuke. Your own heart may need a sign of affection more than a flogging. God's insight might steer you there.

WHAT IS NEEDED HERE?

This brings us to the second question we can ask God: *What does this person (or situation) need?*

Even when a child commits what appears to be a flagrant foul—such as when our son seemingly meant to break his brother's toy truck—unless you're dealing with some sort of pathology, it's helpful to remember that nobody wants to be evil, vindictive, or cruel. Most people don't wake up each morning devising ways to wreck their lives and the lives of the people they care most about. Many times, when someone lets us down, it really was just a mistake. I find that asking *What does this person (or situation) need?* gives me the time (five seconds) and space (a couple of controlled breaths) to ascertain what drove the person to goof. Maybe life was just moving too fast. Maybe expectations weren't as clear as I'd thought. Maybe something else was distracting them. Maybe they were dealing with some other issue or pain.

At one point in my parenting, I realized that I was transferring to my children my deep desire for excellence. I work hard and play hard and devote endless hours to making life run smoothly, and while none of these things is necessarily bad, overemphasizing them can add pressure that really doesn't need to be there. Such was the case for my kids. They'd leave an important school paper in the car that was due that day, and I'd fume. They'd neglect to study thoroughly for a test, and I'd fume. They'd forget to put their belongings away after using them, and I'd fume. On and on it went.

God showed me that by demonstrating grace more often than I was demonstrating aggravation, I might win the hearts of my kids. So I changed my ways. Instead of putting notes in their school lunches that read, "I hope you do well on your quiz!" I'd write, "May your light shine brightly today!" or "You're a great friend! I hope someone sees that today."

God is always at work in the world and in individual hearts. I love asking him what he's up to in the hearts of those I know and love. *What do they need, Father?* I ask him. *What challenges are they dealing with? What problems are they trying to solve?*

HOW CAN I MEET THAT NEED?

The third and final question is a natural offshoot of number two: *How can I meet that need?* As you've likely gathered, I'm a very efficient person. What you might deduce from that statement is that patience isn't my strong suit. Oh, to have my husband's patience. He really is the patience king. Often, when I ask God how I can help meet the needs of my family and friends, I discern the word *patience* in his response.

I like things to move along at a nice clip. I like to run fast. I like to cook fast. I like to talk fast. I like to live fast. The problem here, of course, is that working through setbacks and disappointments doesn't often happen at my preferred rate of speed. So, yes, on many occasions, I am invited to practice patience with life and loved ones, measuring my cadence, slowing my roll.

A friend and I were talking recently about how maybe one sign of spiritual maturity is that you start desiring the character traits you don't yet have. If it's true that God is perfect, that all positive character traits emanate from him—and this is the truth, by the way—then it's surely a noble endeavor to desire each of those traits for ourselves. In this way of thinking, an efficient person like me would long for patience. A thoughtful, patient person might desire efficiency, which I consider the skilled stewardship of time. Strong leaders might desire humility, and meek people might be prompted to lead. Peace lovers might desire sharpened conflict-resolution skills, and disrupters might welcome a little peace.

In any case, when we open ourselves up to God's leading, we can be sure we'll show up in the disappointing situation, whatever it is, with compassion and wisdom to spare.

Choose to Use Words Well

There's a third choice that helps us take God's promised way of escape from losing our cool, and it's that we *choose to use our words well.*

Never once upon asking God for direction have I heard him respond with "Scream your head off, Lauren! Really tell them off . . . don't hold back!"

Hardly.

Ten times out of ten, I am prompted toward manifesting the fruit of the Spirit. I am told to hold fast to peace. I am told to be kind. I am told to maintain a sense of self-control.

Every. Single. Time.

You might say, then, that whenever you and I make the second choice in our lineup—speaking to God, and then actually doing what he says to do—this third one takes care of itself. When I am faithful to ask God for direction and then head off in the direction he's told me to go, I use my words well. I use them to build up the other person instead of tearing them down. I use them to encourage the other person instead of making them feel like a fool. I use them to honor the other person instead of going on the attack. And how quickly problems tend to be resolved, when we speak words of gentleness, of kindness, of peace.

Several months ago, our son Jalen was having a rough day. Because of scheduling challenges related to the pandemic, he was doing school online. I set him up in the kitchen so that I could be present if he needed help, but whenever I'd leave the room, the temptation to switch from schoolwork to computer games overtook him, and he'd sneak in some goof-off time. After a few rounds of catching him in this deception, I was pretty annoyed.

"I'm tired of walking by and seeing that you are playing games," I said. "It's schooltime now, not playtime. Please give your teacher your attention."

Suffice it to say, things weren't panning out the way Jalen had hoped. He was bored with online school. He felt like his teacher was blabbing on about things that didn't matter to him. He was frustrated that his mom had caught him doing the opposite of what he was supposed to be doing. And yet I have to give my son credit: he chose wisely in spite of all that.

Later that morning, after Jalen had finished his schoolwork, he poked his head outside where I was watering plants and said, "Mom, are you staying out there awhile?" I asked why he wanted to know, but *poof!* He'd disappeared back into the house.

Twenty or so minutes later, when I was heading back inside, I found a note on the door. It said, "Dear Mom, I'm sorry I played games instead of doing my work. Thanks for caring for me and putting food on the table. I know that I'm lucky, because God gave me a wonderful mom."

Talk about a way to melt a mother's heart.

I went into the kitchen, and there sat a little tray with brunch on it. Scrambled eggs. A toasted blueberry bagel. Mint-flavored hot chocolate in a Sandra Boynton cartoon mug. It felt like Christmas morning. "*Jalen*," I swooned. "What a sweet, sweet thing to do."

"I put a note on the other door, too," he said, beaming, "in case you came in that way instead."

. . .

"I'm sorry."

"Let me see if I've got this right."

"Can you help me understand . . . ?"

"I'm feeling frustrated and should probably take a few deep breaths."

"Can I have a moment to collect my thoughts?"

"How can I help?"

"What do you need?"

"Can I pray for us both right now?"

These are all great things to say when you're feeling a little let down by life: words of kindness, words of thoughtfulness, words of peace.

You and I both can get steadier—I know this to be true. We can take life as it comes to us. We can weather each storm that we face.

8

LONG-HAUL LIVING

Choose Perseverance

Lauren

I'm a decent runner today, but I didn't start out that way. As with most people, my first attempts at running felt like a major form of punishment. My body wasn't sure what was happening, my breathing struggled to regulate, and despite how far my brain thought I could go, my legs kept screaming to stop and go home. But then a funny thing happened. Ask any faithful runner, and you'll hear the same story time and again: one day, things just clicked. I fell into a sustainable rhythm, my breathing normalized, and I started *wanting* to run. Not because I felt obligated or guilted by my running group but simply because running brought me joy.

Still today, I feel free when I run. The *Chariots of Fire* guy had it right: I feel connected to God when I run, and to his

creation, and to the delight he takes in my life. I feel empowered. I feel light on my feet. I feel *good*. So I run. I run alone.
I run with my friends. I run whenever I have an unassigned
half hour. I run as much as I can. And these days, I never give
my breathing a second thought. Whenever I start running,
my lungs just know what to do. I never give my legs a second
thought either. Whenever I start running, they kick into gear.
What was once arduous is now automatic. I'm a runner. I'm
someone who runs.

The more years I live, the more I realize that not just in
recreational activities such as running but, rather, in *all* of life,
what we practice is who we become. Tony touched on this idea
in his chapter on integrity, and I, too, find it to be true. What
you and I do in this hour impacts how this day will be spent.
And how this day winds up being spent impacts how our week
goes. And how this week goes dramatically influences how we
feel about this month, which absolutely tips our perception of
the entire year. Stack a few years together and a few years after
that, and eventually we've got the sum of our life. I don't say this
to put undue pressure on any one decision. I say it to encourage us in our pursuit of excellence. Without exaggeration, one
excellent decision made today can positively alter the course of
our lives.

Makes me think twice about that supersize order of fries—
you, too?

. . .

In the last chapter, we looked at a few straightforward choices
we can make in hopes of becoming steadier people, people who
can more easily deal with the bumps in the road that threaten

to trip us up in everyday life. Those choices were to receive reality as it arrives, talk to God, and use our words only to encourage—to build up—other people. I told you that a big reason I care so deeply about making these three choices as often as possible is that I've seen what happens when people don't live this way: over time, their sense of entitlement devolves into outright bitterness, and like poison, it takes their lives—or their liveliness, anyway.

What I didn't yet address is what happens when people do make these choices—moment by moment, day by day, year after year after year. These people are blessed indeed, because what happens to the one who keeps choosing steadiness is that they *learn to persevere.*

One of the most popular passages of Scripture on the topic of perseverance is James 1:2-3, which says, "Consider it pure joy, my brothers and sisters, whenever you face trials of many kinds, because you know that the testing of your faith produces perseverance" (NIV).

These verses always cause trouble for people because the sentiment seems so opposed to how we generally experience life. Who wants to think about trials as "joy"—let alone "pure joy"? Our minds can't wrap themselves around such an idea. Trials feel inconvenient, unwelcome, annoying, painful, and bleak. They don't even live in the same *universe* as joy.

But then there's that "because," which tips us off to James's plan to tell us the method to his madness. We aren't to consider trials joyful because we are interested in harming ourselves; we are to consider them joyful because it is only by those trials that we learn to persevere. And according to the next verse, James tells us that when we "let perseverance finish its work," we will be people who are "mature and complete, not lacking anything" (v. 4, NIV).

Another translation says we will be "perfect and complete, needing nothing" (NLT).

Whichever words you want to use, I say yes and amen to that promise. Perfect. Mature. Complete. Lacking nothing. These are words I think of when I envision our eternal dwelling place at God's side in heaven. To think that we could experience such a reality here on earth is more than most people can imagine. Yet God's promise, coming to us courtesy of James, stands. When we choose "cheerful constancy," which is what the word translated *perseverance* means in the original Greek version of James 1:3, we experience spiritual completeness that the rest of the world doesn't know.

In the context of marriage, I love that Tony and I have been married for thirty-nine years, because it has only been by making it to that anniversary that we were able to learn things we didn't know at any of the previous ones. And as we continue on in our union, I love knowing that what I learn this year and next year and the next year after that will be gifts I'm able to unwrap only because I chose to stay married to him. In this case, my choice is easy—perhaps the easiest I make day by day. For other choices, great courage is required . . . but it's courage incredibly well spent. The blessings of perseverance are reserved for those who persevere, which means that when we *do* persevere, we are mightily blessed.

. . .

It's worth pausing here to state what may be obvious to you already, which is that the flip side of the perseverance coin is also true. In the same way that when we let perseverance finish its work, we will be mature and complete, not lacking in anything, when we *don't* let perseverance finish its work, we will be *immature* and *incomplete*, lacking in *everything* . . . or *something*, anyway. You've probably known people along the way who fit this description. Maybe you would have even described yourself that way at some point in your life's journey, as someone who handled setbacks poorly and could never quite figure out why life seemed like it was perpetually out to get you, or why you seemed to be a target for challenging situations even as the rest of the world just cruised along.

The answer might be here: if our expectation is that life will be comfortable and easy all the time, then of course we will feel deeply wronged when things don't go our way. But if we adopt this idea that James talks about, which is to treat trials as sources of *joy*, then not only will we not feel wronged as challenges surface, but we might actually find ourselves *pleased*.

I know that James says "joy," and that "pleased" is somewhere south of joy. But even *pleased* may be too strong of a word for how trials make us feel right now. We must work our way into this concept gently, though, or we'll reject it before we've given it a chance. To do that, I'm going to tell you a bit more about my son Jordan's story, and how his choices in life point to the power and possibility of experiencing joy in the face of tough times.

· · ·

"You need to return this baby to the agency."

Those were the first words the doctor said to me upon completing a medical examination of my brand-new baby boy,

Jordan. "You don't want to be saddled with this," he continued, dropping my heart down into my shoes.

I sat in the exam room dumbfounded, my eyes alternately darting between Jordan, who was in my arms, and the doctor, who sat five feet away. Was he serious? He wanted me to give this baby back?

Perhaps because my mouth couldn't form words, the doctor continued, "He will be nothing but problems, Mrs. Dungy. You'll be running around to doctors' appointments every day, and you are too busy already to be dealing with that. This baby's needs will take over everything. He will negatively impact your marriage. And your relationship with your other three children. Really. Don't wait. Call the adoption agency now, and tell them you've changed your mind. Tell them you'll bring him back before the end of the day."

With every sentence this doctor spoke, my heart was breaking a little more. I'd already bonded with Jordan. I already loved him. I wasn't about to "turn him back in."

I looked at the doctor and said, "I want to be the one who helps him. I want to be the one who walks through life with him. I want to be the one who celebrates each of his accomplishments with him. I don't want to let anyone else fill that role."

Actually, now that I'm replaying this entire situation twenty-one years after the fact, I can't recall if I said all that or just thought it. Either way, I meant it. I meant it from deep in my soul.

. . .

Jordan's parents were responsible college students. They were young—too young, in their own estimation, to raise a child—but they did everything they could to set up Jordan for success.

For starters, his birth mother made the courageous decision to give her baby life instead of aborting him. She went to each of her prenatal appointments. Like every mama, she hoped that she would deliver a perfect child—ten fingers, ten toes, bright eyes, beautifully functioning organs and senses, all just as it should be. At two days old, it was apparent to everyone looking that this baby had his own definition of "perfection." He'd carve his own distinct path in this world.

Minutes after Jordan's birth, when a nurse raised the dropper and let antibacterial drops fall into his eyes, Jordan didn't react. The nurse was curious because babies usually cried or screamed. It's not that the drops hurt; it's that *everything* feels invasive when you've been living inside a womb. Later that hour, another nurse described my son as "floppy," explaining that Jordan's joints seemed overly limber somehow. Within weeks, Jordan had accidentally scratched his face raw without ever registering pain. Instead, with each new scratch, he'd stare blankly into space and almost grin, as though something felt pleasant to him. There was a jellylike quality to his entire being—to his expression, to his movements, to his frame.

"God doesn't make mistakes," Tony kept reminding me as the reality of our situation grew roots.

I'm going to use this entire situation to glorify God, I told myself. *This child is not an accident. This child deserves a bright future. This child needs an advocate. I'm going to be here for this child.*

This may sound a little woo-woo, but the moment I made that commitment before God, it was as if a divine flow of energy was turned on somewhere that still hasn't turned itself off. I had energy to see—really see—Jordan's needs. I had energy to manage all the necessary doctors' appointments. I had energy to deal with scheduling specialist after specialist. I had energy to keep explaining his predicament—to medical personnel and friends and family and neighbors and people at church and people at Target—again and again and again.

We started at the Shriners hospital for children here at the University of South Florida, thinking maybe someone local could help. Test upon test was run, and yet no answers were to be found. Next was The Johns Hopkins Hospital in Maryland, and there we found what we sought. "Your baby has CIPA," came the diagnosis. CIPA stands for congenital insensitivity to pain with anhidrosis.

"What does that mean?" I asked the doctor delivering this news to Tony and me.

"He doesn't feel pain and he doesn't sweat," the doctor answered. "Life will be tough for him."

To the first issue: without the ability to register pain, a person will keep on hurting himself, which is exactly what we saw with our boy. Jordan might sit in a weird way and break his arm and have no idea that it was injured. He could bend his finger completely backward and have no clue that it sprained. He could reach for something he had no business touching—a sharp edge, for example—and suffer no pain for the gross misstep. Already, he would sometimes convulse for minutes on end, with no explanation to be found. One morning, I looked at my baby boy, really took him in, and wondered what life would hold for him.

"We don't have a lot of information on this disease," the doctor at Johns Hopkins had told us. "Patients and their families are generally so overwhelmed by the numerous procedures and surgical appointments this disease necessitates that at some point along the way, they give up."

"Well, then what happens?" I'd asked him.

"The baby—the child—just dies."

I fell to the floor and wept that day.

It wasn't what I'd expected to hear.

• • •

It was then that we began to pray. We'd been praying every day, of course. But there is prayer, and then there's *prayer*. We were in this thing now, we knew. On our way out of his office, the doctor had said to us, "Just love on him and enjoy him, because this baby isn't going to make it. If he gets to six years old, well, that will be pure luck."

I was enraged. Calmly, silently enraged. I don't believe in luck. Furthermore, how *dare* that doctor put a limit on what God wanted to do through this child? I redoubled my efforts to get Jordan to seven years of age. Six years just wouldn't do.

Over time, Jordan dented, damaged, or fractured nearly every part of his body, necessitating splints or casts from head to toe. He was hospitalized on countless occasions—for viruses, for infections, for breaks. And then there were the surgeries—more than one hundred and counting today. But at every turn, I went back to that original commitment: *God, use this to bring glory to yourself.*

Eventually we came to view our son's surgeries as a sort of mission field, always seizing the opportunity to draw in medical staff for our family's pre-op prayer time. We'd pray our hearts out in the hallway outside the OR and then pace the waiting-room floor down to its joists.

Five years old.

Six.

Seven.

Jordan had beaten the odds. Who knew if they were the odds, anyway? Perceptions can be foggy at best. He wasn't verbal, but he was content. He was content and insightful and smart.

When he was sixteen years old and taking a class online, I remember happening by him, busy at work. It occurred to me that I'd forgotten to worry about him for some time. He was *thriving*. He was Miracle J.

• • •

"Mom, how is Johnny doing?" Jordan asked me one time. Our family's friend Johnny had had surgery, and Jordan had been thinking about him, longing for news.

I answered my boy's question, but my thoughts were else-where. *Don't you know that the whole world would give you a giant pass on compassion, given all that your body's been through?*

Hidden in my supposition is a powerful truth about Jordan: his body's struggle isn't all there is to know about him. His challenges don't define who he is.

• • •

Another scene comes to mind. Jordan was ten or eleven years old, and we'd just adopted Justin, who was a newborn. To make that situation work, I'd typically strap Justin to my back in one of those baby-wrap situations so my hands were free to push Jordan's wheelchair. We were walking in some parking lot one time, and Jordan craned his neck toward me and said, "Mom, if I scoot over a little, I have the perfect spot for Justin."

My throat hitched. It was so *Jordan*, always looking for ways to accommodate others, to bless those who were in his life.

This was the same kid who, three or four years prior, had decided to support his brother Eric in his football career. Jordan would never be able to play organized sports, but instead of sulking, he chose to serve. Eric had a workout every day, and Jordan took it upon himself to make sure all of Eric's gear was intact. He'd fill Eric's water bottles. He'd make Eric's lunches. He'd pull Eric's bag together so that Eric would be totally prepared.

"What are you doing?" I once asked Jordan, before I knew this was going to be a habit.

"Eric needs these things," Jordan explained to me. "I want to make sure he has everything he needs."

It was then that our family took to lovingly calling Jordan "Mr. Mom." He's often a more efficient one than I am.

. . .

If you were to google the condition Jordan suffers from, you'd find agonizing photos of people with greatly enlarged joints, stunted fingers and toes, misshapen limbs, open ulcers and wounds, and other visible signs of trauma that can't be quickly explained away. Yet when Tony and I look at our son, now an adult, we see nothing but *life*. We see achievement. We see accomplishment. We see triumph. We see deep progress, step by step.

I think back on Jordan's graduation from high school, an event no medical expert said would be possible for our son. In fact, Jordan had just completed a two-month hospital stay and was discharged the day before the ceremony was set to occur. School officials had peppered parents of graduating seniors with clear communication regarding expected etiquette during the ceremony—and for good reason, as there would be hundreds upon hundreds of graduates honored that day. The last thing the school needed was a stadium filled with people acting up.

Did I obey those rules of etiquette?

I absolutely did not!

I'd packed a bag full of noisemakers and poppers, one for each member of our massive Dungy contingent, and was quite pleased with myself for getting past the security-checkpoint woman, who eyed the contents of my overflowing handbag with more than a little suspicion. I smiled broadly and shrugged as if to say, *What's a proud mom to do?* to which she responded with a knowing shake of her head.

An hour later, when the emcee read Jordan's full given name aloud and our boy started hobbling his way across that platform—*without* a wheelchair, I might add—our section erupted in praise. We yelled Jordan's name. We whistled. We whooped and hollered. We laughed and cried and cheered and blew our oh-so-loud noisemakers and were the absolute definition of obnoxious. Guess what: *we did not care.* We were so proud! Given what that young man had been through, he deserved an outright parade, a dozen marching bands, a fireworks show dedicated just to him. He deserved the cheers of ten thousand voices. He deserved to feel seen and celebrated and loved. And I dare say he felt just that.

I think back on all the times Jordan's head was completely swathed in bandages from some surgery or procedure, and when he noticed that onlooking children were curious, he'd smile, wave them over, and say, "It's okay. You can touch them if you want."

He welcomed their curiosity. He welcomed their questions. He welcomed their incredulity over the things he'd endured.

When I look at Jordan now, I think about when he overcame the elbow issue that almost cost him his arm. This was two, almost three years ago, and I remember praying every night, "Lord, I know you say you're in control and that you can and will handle every situation we face, but please don't let Jordan lose his arm."

Jordan needed a risky surgery, and his surgeon kept saying to Tony and me, "I hope we don't lose the arm . . ."

The doctor was worried.

Tony and I were worried.

Our entire family was worried.

Jordan just kept on keeping on.

Following the surgery, the doctor came out to update us. "All I can say is that it was a miracle. I'm thrilled to tell you that the arm is fine."

I think about how socially active Jordan is today versus when he was younger. As a small child, he never had friends. He was easily overwhelmed by even midsize gatherings and seemed most relaxed when surrounded by our nuclear family and no one else. At some point during his teenage years, that all changed. Jordan became a social magnet. His friends constantly came over to watch sports on TV or to play basketball in the driveway, with Jordan as referee.

These days, Jordan and his friends like to take over the kitchen, whipping up one delectable dish or another, based on what they last saw on their favorite Food Network shows.

Whenever Tony and I get ourselves in a bind because of busy schedules, those same friends are the ones who offer to accompany Jordan to his frequent doctor's appointments in Palm Beach, which is a six-hour round-trip drive from Tampa. And that's without the time spent in the appointment itself. Jordan's pride and joy is his new Ford F-150, which he bought with his own hard-earned money, but after being poked and prodded and interviewed and assessed for six or seven hours during those appointments, the only thing he wants to do is go through the Taco Bell drive-thru, fill his belly with fast food, and crash there in the passenger seat. One of his friends is always happy to drive him home.

Otherwise, that young man is *always* behind the wheel. He had to have surgery on his right foot and ankle one time, and instead of laying off driving during the weeks he was recovering, he developed this unorthodox—and probably terribly unsafe—method of crossing his feet and using his left foot to push the pedals. I'd try to drive him to all the places he needed to be, and at one point, he looked at me and said, "Mom, you have been running like crazy all day. You go relax in the passenger seat and let me do the driving."

Ironically, Jordan using his left foot is a better driver than 95 percent of the population using their right. He's cautious. He's courteous. He's calm. Admittedly, he could stand to pay a little closer attention to that gas gauge of his, but otherwise, I've got no complaints.

I think of Jordan working diligently as a server at 4 Rivers Smokehouse, a restaurant here in Tampa, delivering platter after platter of those delicious burnt ends with beans, potato salad, and collard greens with ham. Being around a commercial kitchen makes him irrationally happy. I always wonder if he'll have his own place someday. . . .

All that to say, we look at this wise, winsome, hilarious, servant-hearted son of ours, and the *last* thing we think of is a diagnosis, a prognosis, a disability, or a disease. We see a godly young man who, in the face of unbelievable and innumerable obstacles, has displayed cheerful constancy every time. He has practiced choosing steadiness so often that he now knows no other option than to wholeheartedly persevere.

We pray for his full and complete healing. We still pray that prayer every day. But until then, until God takes away his physical ailments and gives his body vitality it's never known, we praise God for the things Jordan *has* been able to do. And, of course, we praise him for the person Jordan has become.

. . .

It's not a reach to see Jordan's CIPA condition as a sort of thorn in the flesh, to quote the apostle Paul. Despite Paul's impactful thirty-five-year public ministry, he was plagued by what he called a "thorn in my flesh" (2 Corinthians 12:7). In that same chapter of Scripture, Paul wrote of the revelations he'd received from God but said he wouldn't boast about them because he didn't want to shine the spotlight on himself. Then he went on: "So to keep me from becoming proud, I was given a thorn in my flesh, a messenger from Satan to torment me and keep me from becoming proud" (v. 7).

Speculation abounds regarding the nature of this thorn. Was it Paul's poor eyesight? Was it epilepsy or chronic migraines? Was it malaria? Was it a speech impediment? We never learn what Paul's exact thorn was, but we do learn that, on three separate occasions, he begged God to take it away.

It was never taken away.

"Each time," Paul wrote in 2 Corinthians 12:9-10, "[the Lord] said, 'My grace is all you need. My power works best in weakness.' So now I am glad to boast about my weaknesses, so that the power of Christ can work through me. That's why I take pleasure in my weaknesses, and in the insults, hardships, persecutions, and troubles that I suffer for Christ. For when I am weak, then I am strong."

Paul's thorn was more than distracting; it was devastating.

It was also an instrument of divine power in his life.

Our setbacks can become our superpowers when our lives are centered on the grace of God.

Which brings me to a question: What is the "thorn" you wish would be removed from your life but, day after day, is still there? Is it a financial thorn that keeps poking you, reminding you that regardless of how much money you make, you'll always have debt weighing you down? Is it a relational thorn jabbing you, telling you you'll never find "the one"? Is it an emotional thorn that pricks your moment-by-moment reality, keeping you crouched there, wrapped in fear? Is it a mental thorn that torments you, threatening to shroud you in darkness for life?

These thorns that so many of us deal with in life remind us that the way life unfolds really and truly is so often outside of our control. They remind us that we are incapable in our own strength to bear up under the pain and discomfort they bring. And they remind us that God's purposes are often accomplished via means we would not choose. But they also point to something more profound than these reminders, which is that those of us who suffer from the greatest weakness get to be those who know the greatest strength.

I see this strength in my son Jordan. Tony and I often shake our heads in amazement over the noble choices he makes. How does he have a seemingly bottomless supply of energy for serving others? How can he be so cheerfully others-focused? Why does it seem easier for him to quietly, humbly go about his business than it does for the rest of us, when *he* is the one in greater need? How is he always able to see his siblings' needs—and start meeting them!—before they even recognize the needs themselves?

At this point, twenty-one years into Jordan's life, I'm onto him. The reason I see so many similarities between my boy and Jesus himself is that they've tapped into the same source of strength. And when God is fueling your existence, you care more about serving others than about being served. You invest yourself more fully in meeting others' needs than in tending to your own. You enjoy a certain maturity.

A certain completeness.

A life lacking nothing.

9

PUSHING PAUSE

Choose Rest

Tony

Around the NFL, the idea of commitment often equates to how willing you are to give your entire life over to the sport. Players are seen as committed only if they devote 100 percent of their time to studying the game, playing the game at a very high level, and getting better and better each week. Coaches are seen as committed only if they work upward of eighty hours a week facilitating those player objectives. And whenever a player raises the bar on commitment by, say, showing up in the weight room at 3 a.m., or a coach raises the bar on commitment by sleeping in his office night after night, it seems the bar gets raised on everyone else as well. Whatever level of commitment they were showing to the game is now not quite enough, and so a fresh level of obsessiveness takes hold.

I've seen this trend in other industries as well. It's the CEO who hasn't had a vacation in ten years. It's the entrepreneur who regularly logs fourteen-hour days. It's the pastor who is waiting until his work is finished before he takes a real break.

The problem with that approach, of course, is that church work is never done.

In every profession, there is a real risk of burnout when we refuse to pause from time to time and rest. I saw it in players who didn't know how to recover during the off-season. They'd come back depleted before we played the first game of the next season—not to mention far more vulnerable to injury. I saw it in coaches who didn't know how to go home. After a few years of overworking, their *insides* became overworked. They'd suffer health issues. They'd break down emotionally. Their marriages would start to erode.

You might be able to go ninety miles an hour for a few seconds, but try to sustain that pace for a couple of decades, and inevitably you're going to crash. I've seen it too many times to count: when we are unwilling to stop on our own, life has a way of stopping us. And the catastrophe that ensues is always devastating to watch.

• • •

When I met Coach Noll, I was a twenty-one-year-old who'd never been around professional sports. I played for him and then coached for him, and that decade represented all that I knew of the game. To this day, it remains one of the most significant blessings in my life, having been mentored by one of the greats. It wasn't until I left Pittsburgh that I realized not everyone does things the way Coach Noll did. This was true regarding dozens of subjects, but one of the more memorable ones was *rest*.

Coach always beat the same drum regarding rest for us players. "Get away from this building," he'd say. "Go spend time with your family. Go engage with the community. Go do something completely different from what you do when you're here. Don't say you're taking the day off but then spend the day watching game film or lifting weights. Leave football behind on your days off. It will still be here when you get back."

This mentality supported Coach's initial injunction to not let football become our lives. He knew what we couldn't yet wrap our minds around, which was that, despite football feeling like the most important part of our world at the time, the day would come—and for most of us, sooner rather than later—when we'd say goodbye to the sport we loved so much. He wanted us to have something left at the end of our football careers. He wanted us to still have a *life*.

On Friday afternoons, Coach would insist that his staff go find something to do. What's more, as we were all heading out each week, he'd holler, "Don't call in! Do not check in!"

He wasn't going to be in the office, so he didn't want us there either. He had every intention of unplugging and relaxing, and he wanted us to do the same. He was a fantastic role model on how to maintain a healthy rhythm in life—working hard but resting hard too—and once I became a head coach, I sought to implement what I'd learned.

In Tampa, I caught some heat from fans that first year, who alternately blamed our 6-10 record on my communication style (I didn't "amp up" enough for them) and on the fact that for the Bucs, Saturdays were "family day." But years later, when our

Indianapolis team won the championship, I had to chuckle over the fact that I still hadn't screamed or cursed, and Saturdays had still been family day.

Family day was a tradition I'd picked up from Coach Noll, who'd implemented it successfully for twenty-three years. On Saturday mornings, our team's family members would show up at the practice facility, and kids were allowed onto the field with their dads to watch the drills. During the season, wives and children sacrificed so much time for the sake of the team that it felt important to connect them to the process each week in a fun, honoring way. Families loved it. Players loved it. (Well, most of them. Peyton gave me grief season after season, saying we should use Saturdays for hard-core practice time. I laughed when, years later, I was in Denver to interview him for NBC and learned that he'd been giving the Broncos head coach John Fox grief for *not* letting Saturdays be family days. Once he and his wife had children, he saw the value of those kid-friendly times.)

In all honesty, I loved it too. Something in me knew that I was routinely getting better production out of those fifty-three men by forcing a little downtime than I would have had I pushed them seven days a week. Study after study supports my hunch here. We are more productive when we are rested. We work *harder* (and also smarter) after a day of rest.

● ● ●

As in all of life, I take my cues on establishing a healthy work/rest rhythm from the themes I find in the Bible. It's impossible to look at the life of Jesus and not see him prioritizing the practice of rest. Obviously, he worked diligently, spreading the Good News of the gospel through his preaching, teaching, and healing ministry. He also made a point of engaging with the individuals he came across. But he was known to pull away from time to time, to retreat, to remove himself from his obligations, to *rest*.

I always picture him saying to his disciples, "Guys, these crowds are wearing me out. Let's get out of here and take a breather. We'll come back better, stronger, if we do." I know Lauren told you about our son Jordan in the last chapter. The image I'm picturing here is of Jordan fighting the good fight each day of his life but then falling fast asleep on his way home from every surgery, every procedure. There's a time to fight, for sure. But there's also a time to let that Taco Bell stupor have its way, lay back your seat, and rest.

. . .

Lauren and I have always been active people, filling our days to overflowing, always juggling a dozen balls. Simultaneously, we've always been serious about rest. We don't view rest as sacrificing productivity; we view it as *empowering* us to be productive. While we do begin our days in a restful way by praying together, and we invest our off-season Sundays in restful ways by going to church and then spending the day at home, the most impactful rhythm of rest we've known in the last decade wasn't something we pursued but rather something that seemed to pursue us.

In 2010, our son Eric began playing football for the University of Oregon, which is located in the picturesque town of Eugene, on the south end of the Willamette Valley. Lauren and I decided that we would prioritize seeing Eric in as many home games as we could swing, which would mean visiting seven or eight times each year. If you follow Oregon Ducks football at all, you know we weren't the only ones who were interested in being at those home games. We quickly discovered that finding hotel rooms for our large family wasn't going to be as easy as we'd hoped.

"What if we found a little place out here?" Lauren asked me one day as we roamed the downtown Eugene streets. Everywhere you turn in Eugene, it looks like you're staring at a postcard. Lauren loved the idea of spending more time in that town, of being able to leave some belongings in Oregon so we didn't have to lug so many suitcases back and forth, and of not having to find hotel rooms for every visit. I agreed.

So throughout the fall and winter of Eric's four years playing ball—2010 through 2013—we made ourselves a little home away from home, a place where, despite having to pack our many children like sardines into tiny bunk rooms, we could gather, support Eric, and rest.

．．．

As I say, the resting part wasn't part of our original plan. It's just that when you head off to a place that by comparison to your usual surroundings is pretty sleepy, a place where none of your obligations can find you, and a place where there is so much fun to be had outdoors, you can't help but feel pretty good. Over time, we started heading to Oregon during the summertime so we could get everything ready for the season to come. The more time we spent in Eugene, the more we wanted to be there. We found our favorite local restaurants. We found a church that felt like home. Lauren and I, as well as our kids, started making new friends. It truly seemed like a dream come true.

One summer morning, I was sitting outside our place, just taking in the view. I had on the same sweatshirt I'd tugged on three days in a row. Lauren and the kids were all roaming around nearby. We had nothing on the day's agenda. And the only sound I heard was *peace*. I couldn't get over the contrast. We love our daily life back in Tampa, but "peaceful" isn't usually our state. School mornings regularly feel like a fire drill. Getting every child to where he or she needs to be each week often necessitates expert-level strategic planning. Things are sometimes moving so quickly that if you stand still, you might get mowed down.

We love the hustle and bustle.

Also true: we love it when the chaos dies down.

In Eugene, it always dies down.

In Eugene, nobody knows who I am . . . or more the case, nobody cares. I remember being delighted the first year Eric played ball that people were far more impressed that I was the dad of a Duck than that I was on national TV.

In Eugene, our dress code is always casual.

In Eugene, our mood is mostly light.

Even after Eric graduated from college, our family kept returning to Eugene. We'd told ourselves we went to Oregon for him, but at some point our motivation shifted. We were going there for ourselves.

. . .

You might be reading this thinking, *Must be nice to be able to uproot your life for weeks on end and head to a different state!*

Or you might instead be thinking, *Eugene? Seriously?* That's *the best you can do?*

Either way, let me say this: our time in Eugene has taught me some things that I believe are relevant to you. I've learned a few truths about prioritizing rest that might help you do the same. Whether you practice these things in Eugene, Oregon, or on a fancy island somewhere, or on the floor of your laundry room while your baby is sleeping because that's the only place where you can be alone, I challenge you to give rest a try and see if it serves you well.

LESSON 1: REST REQUIRES PREPARATION

If you've ever known someone who is of the Jewish faith, then you know they are very intentional about practicing the Sabbath every week. For the Jewish people, Sabbath lasts from sundown on Friday until sundown on Saturday, and during those hours, they are careful not to work. This means that all preparations for their Sabbath time must be made before Sabbath begins. Food must be purchased, prepared, and cooked. The house must be clean. Supplies must be procured. Arrangements must be made. Because once the sun sets on Friday, the window for preparing has closed.

Given that I wrote an entire chapter for this book on the merits of preparation, you know how I feel about this: in the same way that we prepare for our work, we must take pains to prepare for our rest. Which means, for starters, you've got to schedule your rest.

For some people, the phrase "schedule your rest" is equivalent to saying, "schedule getting the flu" or "schedule your nervous breakdown." Most of us in the United States are so out of practice when it comes to resting that the moment we try to do so, we get sick or come emotionally undone. Please hear me when I tell you that the more you practice resting, the better at resting you'll get.

When Lauren and I lay out our year each January, we tag the weeks we plan to spend in Oregon. And like Jewish people with their weekly Sabbath, we jealously guard those weeks. As the date nears for our departure, we start pulling out children's suitcases and laying out stacks of clothes. Does everyone have a swimsuit that fits? Has anyone lost their hiking boots? Do we need to bring additional supplies that we didn't leave behind last time? And what about books to read?

Lauren bears much of the packing burden each time, so she begins her process days in advance. Once we're in Eugene, we're in Eugene for a *while*. She likes to leave nothing at all to chance.

• • •

When I coached, I felt the same pressure every NFL coach feels, which is to stay on the performance merry-go-round. Pro football is an athletic endeavor, but it's also entertainment. And people never stop wanting to be entertained. Even the year that we won the Super Bowl, once the final piece of confetti had landed on the ground, reporters were at the ready: "So, Coach, looking ahead to next year, do you think the Colts can repeat?"

Enough is never really enough.

If you're not careful, regardless of the work that you do, the people you provide for, or the community of which you're a part, unless you intentionally carve out time to pull away from your world, that world just might eat you alive.

This leads me to a question: Looking ahead from where you sit today, when are you planning to rest? You might be working on a high-stakes project or finishing a massive remodel or wrestling through a relational quandary that is taking every last bit of energy you've got. I understand those things. I've faced similar situations, in fact. But you know as well as I do that unless you've got a break coming on the heels of those pressing issues, a new set will be waiting to take you down.

So when are you scheduled to rest? Even if it's just for a day—or a couple of hours, for that matter—when will you push aside other (useful, necessary) tasks and let yourself come back to life?

If my experience is any guide, then failing to *plan* to rest is failing to rest. If I don't anticipate its arrival and hold fast to those designated days, the rest I so desperately need just isn't going to occur.

Decide today that you're going to start your day tomorrow in a restful place, saying a prayer, maybe, or just lying in bed taking a few centering breaths. Claim those moments for the purpose of rest.

Decide today that this coming weekend, you're going to take a few hours to be outside with loved ones or to listen to that audiobook you've wanted to start. Claim those hours for the purpose of rest.

Decide today that at the next big break in your action—at the end of your kids' school year, perhaps, or after you deliver a big presentation at work or when winter gives way to spring—you're going to take a day to pull away from other obligations and devote yourself to the practice of rest.

Whatever your specific rhythms of rest might include, get your periods of rest scheduled *now*. Anticipate their arrival with enthusiasm, knowing you'll be better, stronger, and *so* much happier as you practice intentionally pulling away.

LESSON 2: REST REQUIRES RESOLVE

Every year, the Dungy side of our family gets together for a massive family reunion. Which means that for the past decade, Lauren, the kids, and I have been absent. It wrecks me to acknowledge this fact because I care deeply about my extended family, I love being with my extended family, and family gatherings with my numerous aunts and uncles and cousins are always a ball. But the weeks that make up July and part of August are the weeks when we are in Eugene each summer, and those weeks have become nearly sacred to Lauren and me. Which brings me to the second lesson I've learned: rest requires resolve.

Once you schedule your hour or day or season of rest, you won't *believe* how many people and things will start vying for that time. It will feel like an evil plot being carried out against you. *Everyone* will have yet one more thing that they need you to attend or participate in or do. Remember that Jewish practice of guarding the Sabbath? Even once you've scheduled your rest, you'll need to jealously guard it all the way through.

If you're like me, here's the temptation you'll face: you'll carve out time to rest, and then someone will need something of you. *Oh, I can come help with that . . . it will only take an hour or two.* You'll leave your restful state to help out one person, but when you return to your scheduled rest, you'll have to start all over again. Pop in and out enough times over the hour or day or week you'd slotted for resting, and you'll get no rest at all.

My advice: cut the distractions from the start. Turn off your phone's notifications. Tell the people you deal with day in and day out that you'll be unavailable for the designated time. Make accommodations for people and situations that may need you while you're away. And then fight like crazy to protect the time you promised yourself was *yours*.

Admittedly, it's easy for me to say no to opportunities that arise back home while I'm in Eugene since I'm a six-hour plane ride away. Even so, I have become so comfortable protecting my times of rest that even when I'm home in Tampa, I have no trouble saying no. Again, this isn't because I'm stingy about showing up and serving. It's because I want to show up and serve for decades to come that I'm so serious about protecting my rest. We can't give what we don't have. I want to give and give and give, until my final day.

LESSON 3: REST RESULTS IN REFUELING

If you've ever lain in bed all night, unable to sleep, then you know there is a vast difference between *stopping* and *resting*. We can cease doing activity. That is called stopping. But lying in bed all night *not* sleeping won't exactly make you feel rested the next day. In the same way, there is more to resting than the ceasing of activity. Just because we stop tending to our normal daily obligations doesn't mean we have experienced rest.

Let me show you what I'm saying. Each time my family heads off to Eugene, it takes us a full day to get there. It takes a few hours to get going at home and drive to the airport. It takes a couple of hours to make our way through the maze of lines and checkpoints and arrive at our gate. It takes six or seven hours to fly to Oregon. And then it takes a while to get our baggage, load up our vehicle, and finally head to the house. It's a sunup-to-sundown endeavor every time.

Not restful yet.

Once we arrive, it takes some doing to get everyone settled.

There are suitcases to unpack, supplies to account for, and sheets to put on beds.

Still not restful.

After that initial unpacking process, we always seem to start our stay with a round of errands. We need food. We need drinks. We need whatever we ran out of last time. And while roaming around downtown Eugene is actually a pretty enjoyable experience, "errands" aren't what I'd call "rest."

But then the next day dawns. Everyone is settled in. We have food. We have drinks. We have supplies. We have each other. And before us, we have a totally obligation-free day. We could go for a hike up Spencer Butte. We could go for a bike ride, just us. We could laze around the house talking or playing games. We could pick berries. We could fire up the grill and invite friends over. We could just sit and stare at a tree. There is nothing we have to do. We can do anything or nothing at all.

Now *this*—this feels like rest.

Being outside, enjoying God's creation, is restful to me because it returns me to a more centered state. Spending unrushed time talking with Lauren and the kids is restful to me because it expands my perspective and deepens my appreciation for them. Sharing a meal with friends as we sit around a campfire and talk about all that we've seen God do in our lives since the last time we were together—that is *always* restful to me because it reminds me what life's really about.

The living of daily life takes a serious toll on every single person who dares to live it. Think carefully about what refuels you, what recenters you, and what refills your tank, so you can be sure to include some of those things during each of your periods of rest.

. . .

I was asked once about the traits I hoped to see emerge in each of my children as they grew up. If I could instill just one or two characteristics into their lives, in other words, which ones would I choose? My answer came in a flash. I hope that every member of my family is known first and foremost as someone who loves and honors God. Since this spiritual part of life is the subject of the next chapter, I'll leave it at that for now and move on to the second part of my response. In addition to being known as people who are devoted to God, I hope my children are known as those who are *devoted to others*, too.

I care far less about the grade my son got on a chemistry test than about his befriending someone who seemed friendless that day.

I care far less about how many shots my daughter made in her team's basketball game than about her helping the coach pick up and organize the gear afterward.

I care far less about the dollar amount of the raise my child received at work than about his proving trustworthy with that money once it's in his account.

I bring these things up because it is only from a place of rest that my children—and you and I, too, for that matter—can become the type of people we long to be. It takes *reserves* to reach out to lonely people. It takes *reserves* to serve when you'd rather go home and relax. It takes *reserves* to exhibit self-control and self-discipline. *Rest* is how we build those reserves.

10

FULL SURRENDER

Choose Jesus

Tony

When we covered the subject of teamwork earlier, I mentioned that we'd tackle the final aspect of the four vital elements that form the *soul* of a team in a later chapter. That chapter has arrived, and that final aspect—the *L*—is *larger purpose*.

Like everyone who is part of the NFL, I agree that winning is fun. Every player or coach worth his bonuses has logged plenty of sleepless hours trying to figure out how to beat one team or another. We all know how to win; it's *doing* it that sometimes presents a problem. But then the elusive victory comes, and instead of basking in our hard-earned success, we look ahead to the next game, determined to win that one too. You see where this goes: even the most successful teams in history couldn't win every game they played. Eventually everyone loses, and then what do you have left?

My friend Herm Edwards, now the head coach for Arizona State, mastered the art of the pithy phrase so deftly that people started referring to his sayings as "Hermisms." Surely the most famous of them is the straightforward phrase "You play to win the game." Seeing it here in print doesn't do it justice; for the full effect, you need Herm's classic phrasing, complete with perfectly placed pauses.

"You *play* . . . to *win* . . . the *game.*"

You know what? Herm's absolutely correct. Who in their right minds would suit up and take the field and put their bodies through the paces like that if not to win the game? In every game I played, we played to win the game. In every game I *coached*, I coached to win the game. Same goes for every other sane person who has been part of this sport.

But also true is that, even for professional athletes and coaches, winning games will never meet our deepest needs. Victories and championships and dynasties cannot satisfy the human soul. It takes a larger purpose to do those things.

• • •

When I arrived in Pittsburgh, ready to secure a spot on the team the late Art Rooney owned, part of what intrigued me from the outset was not his passion for winning but his passion for winning *well.* To Mr. Rooney, *how* we won was as important as *that* we won. He wasn't interested in our being the best football team in the league if it also meant that we'd sold our souls. He wanted the quality of our character as human beings to be every bit as substantive as the quality of our play. And he made sure we upheld that standard too. His childhood home had stood in the neighborhood where Three Rivers Stadium was built in 1970 and where the Steelers played their home games from 1970 until 2000. From 1972 until the end, they sold out every single game, a testament to the incredible fan base Mr. Rooney established in his hometown. The Steelers of that era—throughout the 1970s especially—were known as fighters, and on the field I guess that was true. But as men, the word that comes to mind is *kind*. The majority were caring, servant-hearted men.

Years later, when I was leaving Tampa Bay and heading to Indianapolis to coach the Colts, owner Jim Irsay told me his approach was similar to Mr. Rooney's. Jim grew up watching Mr. Rooney's Steelers and wanted to emulate that culture. He was every bit as serious about elevating excellent character in his staff and players as he was about winning ball games.

The message I took away from both men became something of a mantra for me: *It matters how you win.*

I love that statement because winning is implied. Winning isn't demoted to some inconsequential thing. Winning matters. It matters greatly.

What also matters is how you win.

. . .

My path to playing, coaching, and living with a higher purpose was not what you'd call straight. Whenever I was honest with my players about my boyhood and young-adulthood antics, they took great delight in hearing about the person I used to be. I had a foul mouth. I had an aggressively competitive spirit. I was a follower at best, and my behavior betrayed the state of my heart. In some ways, I was just a typical boy who wanted to play sports, who wasn't all that interested in school, and who desperately longed to fit in. But compared with many kids, I did have an advantage: I had parents and grandparents who loved me, who were happily present in my life, and who worked hard to teach me the ways of God.

In the home of my youth, Sundays were reserved for church. Each week, I'd sit with my mom, my dad, and my siblings, and while it was tempting to let my thoughts drift to what I thought were more interesting subjects—football, basketball . . . over time, girls—I didn't dare. I needed to pay attention because I knew my mother and father would be asking questions later about what we'd heard. They wanted to be sure that my siblings and I understood the Scriptures and what was involved in the Christ-following life.

I didn't yet. But my parents were determined to plant seeds anyway, under the assumption that one day they'd bear fruit.

I was nine years old when I raised my hand in response to the preacher asking if anyone wanted to come forward following the service to pray to receive Jesus, and I meant it. The offer of heaven instead of hell sounded great to me, so I walked right up to the altar and prayed exactly what I was told to pray, confessing my sins, acknowledging Jesus as my Savior, determining to go a new way in life. I understood what I was doing academically. I knew what I was doing spiritually. It's just that, practically speaking, I hadn't quite sorted out what "full surrender" might mean for me. That part would take some time.

For the next decade or so—throughout middle school, high school, and most of college—I was so focused on my athletic career that I didn't give my walk with Jesus that much thought. I hung out with my friends, and some of them were believers, but the reason I was a "good kid" throughout those years—aside from my word choice from time to time—had less to do with wanting to please God than it did with not wanting to upset my mom and dad. From them, I'd learned that there were certain things the Bible said to do and not to do, and even once I was in college and living away from home, I figured those guidelines were as good as any I could come up with myself. I obeyed them without regret. Life seemed to work better that way.

As I entered adulthood, if you had asked people who knew me best what I was like, they probably would have said I was driven. Smart. A decent athlete. Nobody would have said the word *Christian*. They wouldn't have said I was spiritual or that I was the kind of person who cared about pursuing righteousness. I was . . . nice. I kept my nose clean. I did what was expected of me and didn't rock too many boats. This is who I was as I came to the Steelers at age twenty-one: a born-again Christian whose faith was both untested and weak.

Arriving in Pittsburgh was a surreal experience. I wouldn't go so far as to say that I idolized the guys who played there, but I definitely knew who they were. I'd watched them play many games while I was still in high school and then in college, and I was well aware that they were the best in the world at what they did. I knew I'd learn a lot from them about the sport of football. What I couldn't have predicted was how much they'd teach me about life.

Donnie Shell, who played safety for the Steelers from 1974 to 1987, had a more profound impact on my spiritual growth during that era than anyone else in my life. Almost from the first time I met him, whenever he'd see me, he'd ask what I'd read that day. He meant read in my Bible. Most days, I'd have to admit that I hadn't read anything. He'd pause a second and then say, "Well, let me tell you what I read."

He'd then go on to detail the verse or passage he'd focused on, what he thought it meant, and how he planned to live in light of what he'd learned. I was awestruck. Who *was* this guy?

Eventually I picked up my Bible and dusted it off after so many years of neglect and read a few things, just so I'd have something to say when Donnie asked me his question.

Donnie and I became roommates, and I watched him every night as he opened his Bible, read for a while, and then thought and prayed about what he'd read. I saw him do the same thing every morning: read, think, pray. He was always telling someone about what he'd learned, a practice I now know helped him sear those lessons into his mind and heart. Donnie really liked the apostle Paul's exhortation in 1 Corinthians 9:24 that says we should "run to win." Honestly, I'd never heard a Christian say that it was okay to want to win. I was intrigued. We could want that and still follow God?

"Just don't forget the next part," Donnie would caution me. "It says to run to win not the prize that will fade away but the *eternal* prize" (see v. 25). It was one of the greatest takeaways from my time with Donnie and the rest of the strong believers on that Steelers team—J. T. Thomas, Jon Kolb, Larry Brown, John Stallworth, and others: *Whatever you do in life, be sure you're running the right race.*

It wasn't lost on me that the more I learned from those guys about God and the Bible and how to live a spiritually productive life, the smarter my parents seemed. *So that's what they were talking about all those Sunday afternoons when I was a kid.* Finally those seeds my parents had planted were sprouting something fruitful. I was starting to get it. I was starting to spiritually grow.

. . .

To this day, I believe that I was saved the moment I prayed that prayer at the altar when I was just nine years old. The Bible says that once we are part of God's family, we can never be snatched from his hand (see John 10:27-29). But in terms of living life surrendered to Jesus—truly making him the Lord of my life, letting God be the directing force of every single day, trusting him with every decision I needed to make, caring more about pleasing God than pleasing my family or my coaches—well, those things wouldn't happen until age twenty-one. Looking back, that was a good time for my life to start changing. I was in somewhat of a fragile place back then. I hadn't been drafted. I wasn't slated to play the position I wanted to play. I wasn't even sure I'd land a spot on the team. I consider it God's grace that led me to the likes of Donnie Shell. I could have just as easily slid into a friend group that wouldn't have had such an uplifting effect. But that's not at all what happened.

Thankfully, God protected me from that.

To the extent that I was able to play and coach with a larger purpose in mind, I attribute that win to that group of teammates I had with the Pittsburgh Steelers. Those men showed me day in and day out what it means to run the right race while fixing my eyes on the absolute right prize.

. . .

I served as a head coach in the NFL for thirteen years, and at the start of each of those seasons, during our first team meeting I'd tell the men sitting in front of me that I was a follower of Jesus Christ. Granted, most of them knew this about me, reputations preceding us as they do. Still, I said it plainly as a way of explaining my coaching philosophy and approach. I wanted them to understand why I said what I said, did what I did, and behaved the way I behaved. More importantly, I wanted to invite them to join me in playing with a larger purpose too. I had no intention of telling them what their larger purpose should be, but I did find that by explaining what mine was, dialogue started flowing regarding how to find their own.

During follow-up conversations when it was appropriate to do so, I'd ask them reflective questions to try to get to the core of what their larger purpose might be, questions like:

- What gives your life meaning?
- What past experiences have impacted you most, and why?
- What's the best compliment someone could give you?
- How long do you think you'll play football?
- What kind of legacy do you hope to leave?
- What do you need to do during this time in your life to leave that legacy?

I spoke frequently of an image that had captivated me back when I was just a boy: the narrow and broad roads Jesus described. My mother had often talked to my siblings and me about the difference between the two roads. She was a Sunday school teacher and would test out her lessons on us kids each week to be sure the messages she conveyed were clear. She must have taught on the concept of the two roads several times because I can still recall her myriad examples:

"If a thousand kids decided to jump off the Brooklyn Bridge, would you jump too?"

"If your friends decide to use alcohol and drugs and throw their lives away, are you going to throw your life away too?"

"Just because the crowd zigs instead of zags, are you going to zig too?"

We'd answer in unison every time: "Nooo, Mom, we won't."

She'd nod her head in satisfaction. "That's right."

Jesus introduced this language of the narrow and broad roads during the longest sermon he ever preached, the Sermon on the Mount, where he gave his followers and curious people who had gathered around him that day his thoughts on the moral code Christians should live by. "You can enter God's Kingdom only through the narrow gate," he said. "The highway to hell is broad, and its gate is wide for the many who choose that way. But the gateway to life is very narrow and the road is difficult, and only a few ever find it" (Matthew 7:13-14).

When I was new to adulthood and new to the league, I remember looking around to see how life was turning out for the guys who'd picked each of those paths. There were plenty of "broad-road" people on the team, and while things sometimes went really well for them—Super Bowl victories, individual accolades, lots of money coming their way—over time, they'd inevitably get to the end of those wins and be worse off than they'd been before.

There were also lots of "narrow-road" guys, and their journeys were intriguing to me. While it was true that the road they were on didn't always look very exciting, it seemed to take them to a better place. Those people were steadier somehow. They weren't at the mercy of life's ups and downs like the broad-road guys were.

I thought back to when I was fourteen years old. My coach had said, "Hey, as the quarterback, you're the *leader* of this team." I'd recoiled at his assessment. I didn't want to be the team's leader. I wanted to be one of the guys. I wanted to have fun, to be popular, to fit in. As I progressed in football, my goal wasn't only to be popular; now I wanted money, too. I'd seen how much money football players made when they were good, so I set my sights on getting good. A main reason I went to college, in fact, was to make more money. I'd learned that if I had an education, I could demand more cash. I could support a family someday. I could have nice things. So I got an education. But there I was, age twenty-one, rethinking my entire plan. If I kept letting things like fame and fortune motivate me, where would I be in the end?

Each year I coached, I'd talk to my players this way, just like I'm talking with you. I'd ask them to consider which path they wanted to walk on during the years they spent in the league.

Of course, not every guy wanted to talk about deep, spiritual things. On the whole, players were respectful of my beliefs, even as I caught some flak from time to time. An afternoon practice in Tampa comes to mind. I'd been working the guys pretty hard trying to beat a storm that was brewing to the west. I asked one of our assistants to keep an eye on the lightning that kept putting scars in the sky. He assured me we were still a good six miles from any of the action, but players were starting to wonder if maybe their coach had lost his mind.

At one point, one of our defensive tackles hollered at me, "Hey, Coach! You evidently know where you're going when you die, but for those of us who don't, we should probably get inside!"

Of all the players I coached, only one refused to join our pregame and postgame prayer times, which, though optional, were well attended. I count it a gift that he chose to tell me why. When he'd been a young boy, his grandmother fell terribly ill. He prayed for her recovery, but instead of getting better, she died. "I couldn't trust God after that," he told me. "No matter how bad I want to, I still can't."

I still pray for that young man from time to time, though he's not so young anymore. I pray for the same thing I pray for us all, which is that we would come to know God through his Son, Jesus, and that we'd devote our lives to him. Fourth-century theologian St. Augustine wrote in his book *Confessions*, "Thou hast formed us for thyself, [O Lord,] and our hearts are restless till they find rest in thee."[1] You know, we talked about the necessity of rest in the last chapter; to me, this is *ultimate* rest. In the world of pro football, players and coaches generally look to externals to determine how they're doing in life. *Did we win? Did we avoid injury? Did we hit the metrics we set? Is the GM pleased? Is the owner pleased? Will our contract get renewed?* I always wanted the guys I coached to see that accepting the gift of God's grace is like signing a contract with a payout that will never dry up. It's like saying yes to eternal security, the type we keep wishing for here on earth.

Coming into that ultimate type of rest was such a relief for me. I remember how it felt to know that I didn't have to strive anymore. I didn't have to perform to prove my worth. I could rest in God's goodness. I could rest in God's sufficiency. I could rest in God's promise that in him, I was always approved.

. . .

Still today, there is no greater joy to me than knowing I have everything I need to live a life that is pleasing to God. I have

God's Word, the Bible, which lays out his will and ways. I have communication with him through prayer, which helps me know specifically what to do. And I have access to limitless resources for acting on that guidance as I give his Spirit control of my life.

Greater still, I can help my children live this way too. I can help them see that while the broad road is absolutely alluring, it leads to destruction in the end. Hopefully, by my example, they will realize that narrow-road living is the most enthralling, exciting, adventure-packed life there is. What I can do in my own strength as I sit here at sixty-six years old isn't all that impressive. But what the omnipotent, omnipresent, omniscient God of the universe can do through me, as I surrender myself fully to him, is astounding every time.

When our son Eric was making his way through his adolescent years, I often wondered if he absorbed a single word that Lauren and I said. Like all Dungy men, he was pretty quiet, pretty reserved. We would sometimes notice long stretches of silence on his part and find ourselves wondering as parents if we were even *close* to getting it right.

He was in Oregon playing ball, and during his second season made his first touchdown catch. Later, a reporter from the school's newspaper, the *Daily Emerald*, caught up with Eric to interview him. The reporter asked five or six questions, then ended with this one: "Having a dad who's a coach can never hurt a player. What tips did your dad give you that still stay with you today?"

My eyes clouded with tears as I read my son's reply. "There are two things," Eric said. "One was a Bible verse that's kind of his favorite verse and my favorite verse—Matthew 16:26—and it says, 'For what will it profit a man if he gains the whole world and forfeits his soul?' So just, no matter what you're doing off the field, in football, whatever, if you lose your core values, what was the point of doing all that?"

Then Eric told the reporter the second thing: "And just remember that football's just a game. It's fun. You want to work hard and be good, but you've got your family, you've got your faith, you've got schoolwork. So that just kind of puts things in perspective."

All I could think was, *That's it. The kid's got it. He's going to be all right.*

Real life is living not for our glory but for God's.

There's no higher purpose to be found than that.

11

SHINING LIKE STARS

Choose Love

Lauren

For the past decade, summers have included those extended stays in Eugene that Tony told you about, and while I could bend your ear for an hour talking about my favorite parts of those visits, some of the best memories each time center on the simple act of looking up at the night sky. I know that stars don't *actually* shine brighter over Eugene, Oregon, than they do over Tampa, Florida, but from where I'm standing on those cool summer nights, it sure seems like they do. With fewer homes per square mile and fewer businesses dotting the city's landscape, the contrast between the rich navy sky and the glowing constellations seems vastly more striking to me than it does almost any other place on earth.

Whenever I think about how arresting that sight is of the stars just beaming against the night sky, I think of Paul's words to the Philippian church when he told them to "do everything without grumbling or arguing, so that you may become blameless and pure, 'children of God without fault in a warped and crooked generation'" (Philippians 2:14-15, NIV). He said that if they were faithful to live this way, a promise would come true for them: "Then you will shine among them like stars in the sky as you hold firmly to the word of life. And then I will be able to boast on the day of Christ that I did not run or labor in vain" (vv. 15-16).

I love the idea of shining for Jesus against the backdrop of a world that in many regards has lost its way. To be "warped" or "crooked" is to be bent out of shape, to no longer be straight. It is to be defective, to be misaligned. These are such fitting words to describe our culture today, which prizes individualism over living surrendered to God. In the same way that it would sound terrible to listen to a thousand drummers all drumming at the same time to their own beat, there's also outright cacophony, spiritually speaking, when human beings live by their own individual truths.

What was true in the first century, when Paul penned his letter to the believers at Philippi, remains true today: we need stars shining brightly so that people living in darkness can *see*. I know it's in vogue these days to take in the warped patterns of this generation and in response just shrug our shoulders, raise our palms to the air, and say, "Eh, who am I to judge?"

But as I see it, this isn't "shining" at all. This isn't "holding firmly to the Word of life," which is just another way of saying to pay attention to the instruction the Bible gives us, and never to stray from what God says to do.

• • •

Looking at the challenges facing us as a society today, one of the ways you and I can shine like stars is to exhibit *joy*. Cynicism has become so rampant lately that sometimes when I smile at or speak a kind word to a stranger, that person looks at me like I've lost my mind or believes that I'm surely talking to someone else.

We can also shine brightly by being people of *peace*. It seems every day we come up with new ways to divide ourselves from one another. What a tragedy this is! God calls us to be one people, just as he, the Son, and the Holy Spirit are one. Disunity is the *opposite* of the way of Christ.

We can shine like stars by being *pure*—that's for sure. Have you noticed that it's becoming more and more difficult to find "family" shows and movies to watch? Even cooking shows have started going the way of the world, normalizing what God's Word says isn't normal at all. Given the vulgarity that's available through all forms of media, purity definitely stands out.

We can shine for Jesus by being *generous*. In our social media–captivated culture, which elevates self-centeredness and "building a brand," a generous spirit really stands out. Notice how baffled people seem these days whenever you ask a sincere follow-up question or try to pay for their meal. Generosity is refreshing, isn't it? It's like a breeze on an otherwise stifling day.

And then there's *honesty*. I think honesty is a good way to shine like stars too. Even something as simple as saying "I don't know the answer to that question" can help establish yourself as a trustworthy person, someone who realizes it's impossible to know everything all the time. Or what about saying "That was my fault" when it was? Or telling a cashier "I think you undercharged me for that" when he or she did? Honesty is letting "your 'Yes' be 'Yes' and your 'No,' 'No,'" as Jesus said to do in Matthew 5:37 (NKJV). What a powerful way to live.

But there is one way that we can "shine like stars" that Scripture seems to elevate above all others, and according to John 13:33-35, it is *love*. Quoting Jesus after his death, burial, and triumphant resurrection, here is what John wrote: "Dear children, I will be with you only a little longer. And as I told the Jewish leaders, you will search for me, but you can't come where I am going. So now I am giving you a new commandment: Love each other. Just as I have loved you, you should love each other. Your love for one another will prove to the world that you are my disciples."

In one of the apostle Paul's letters to the Corinthian church, we gain insight into what love needs to include. "Love is patient and kind," he wrote in 1 Corinthians 13:4-7. "Love is not jealous or boastful or proud or rude. It does not demand its own way. It is not irritable, and it keeps no record of being wronged. It does not rejoice about injustice but rejoices whenever the truth wins out. Love never gives up, never loses faith, is always hopeful, and endures through every circumstance."

We toss around the word *love* to describe everything from how we feel about pizza and perfume to running shoes and video games and everything in between. But that is not love as the Bible describes it. Real love is not natural for us. We can't exhibit real love on our own.

It isn't easy for us to be patient with people who seem intent on driving us crazy.

It isn't easy for us to "never lose faith," especially when things don't go our way.

It isn't easy for us to be kind to someone who isn't being kind to us.

Recently, one of our younger boys was in a mood. He was upset about something and decided to throw books against the wall to let me know how he felt. I asked him to take a time-out in his room. "You don't *like* me," he said as he stormed off.

Now, my son knows full well that I like him. He knows that I love him, that I'm for him, and that I will never, ever give up on him. But he was hurting, and sometimes we say things when we're hurting that we don't exactly mean. While he was still within earshot, I said, "I do like you, Son. I *love* you. But I don't love what you did with those books."

I don't know how you would feel in that situation, but in my flesh, in my natural person, seeing my child misbehave and act so rudely makes me want to throw a few books against a wall myself! It was only by God's grace and by his Spirit's empowerment that I could react to this child's aggression with peace. It was only by his grace that I could absorb my son's anger and choose to manifest love in response.

He still had to spend some time in his room. But at least while he was in there, he knew that he was loved.

In your life and in mine, we will experience countless "book-throwing" incidents, times when people are misbehaving, harming themselves and others, testing our patience, and disrupting our day. As we encounter each of these situations, we have a choice to make. Will we react from our flesh, from our "natural" state? Or will we choose to love?

I don't always make the right choice in these moments, but I count it a great victory that at least these days I know which is the right one to make. For the follower of Jesus, the right choice is *always* love. Admittedly, we don't have to love the book-throwing . . . we shouldn't love it, in fact. But we are called to love the book-thrower, understanding that as he or she surrenders more fully to Jesus, that book-throwing identity will change.

. . .

When thinking about love, it's helpful to consider that because love is a divine attribute, it allows us to do divine things. For example, when we choose to demonstrate love, we can react to people the way Jesus reacted to people when he was here on earth—by stopping to truly see them, by serving them, by sacrificing for them, and so forth. In these ways, we can "hold space" for people as they make their way toward God and commit to full devotedness to him. We can trust that, as we patiently love people right where they are, their spiritual potential will be realized.

We need not compromise our standards of righteousness to love others well. We need not start redefining truth. From our place of wholeness and (hopefully) ever-deepening holiness, we can encourage others, we can pray for others, and we can love them with the love of Christ. We can do this because God's Word tells us that it's his Spirit who brings people into relationship with him; that work isn't ours to do. His job is saving people. Our job is loving them well.

I would also say that when we are careful to honor and bless the person and not the person's "book-throwing" behaviors, we honor the work of God in that person's life. In Galatians 2:20, Paul wrote, "My old self has been crucified with Christ. It is no longer I who live, but Christ lives in me. So I live in this earthly body by trusting in the Son of God, who loved me and gave himself for me."

Everywhere we turn today, we find people and groups who are elevating others' behavior, identity, or lifestyle and calling that "love." This is not a loving thing to do because once a person steps into a surrendered relationship with Jesus, Jesus changes that person in full. The "old self" gets put to death. The "old self" is suddenly *gone*. To the extent that we praise a person's pattern of behavior that is not in alignment with God's will and ways, we distract that person from looking forward with eager anticipation to the "new life" Christ has for him or her. To lean on the example of my son who threw books, this approach is about as useful as it would have been for me to look at him after he misbehaved and say, "Well, you just do you. If you want to be a book-thrower today, then you just be a book-thrower. In fact, if you want to spend your whole *life* being a book-thrower, then so be it. But hey, could you try not to hit the baby we're fostering this week?"

God has established boundaries for his children that help their lives function well, and we are wise to heed those boundaries if we hope to honor him.

So we choose love. We learn the Scriptures. We faithfully practice prayer. We establish systems that help us to honor God. And then we shine like stars in the darkness, loving the world Jesus came to save.

. . .

Based on all that I've told you about my mom, it probably won't surprise you to read that, in my opinion, Doris Harris was about the most loving person this world has ever seen. She was a love pro, through and through. She was the epitome of 1 Corinthians 13:4-7. She was humble. She was considerate. She was other-focused with each person who crossed her path. She was calm under pressure. She was patient during trials. She was forgiving. She was a fierce advocate for truth. She persevered. She kept the faith. Even after losing her father when she was a young girl, she held fast to hope. She endured when lesser people would have caved, always sharing the gospel, always leading Bible studies, always helping young people learn how to devote themselves to God, always preparing meals for people living in group homes, always writing notes of encouragement to people in our church who'd faced loss. She was *exceptional* at loving, and she was careful to pass along to me what she'd learned. Lesson number one was that love is not a noun but a verb.

I'm not sure there was ever a lesson number two.

Love equaled action for my mom, every day, every time.

Still today, as I go through the dailiness of life, I think about what she would do. *What does love require of me right now?* This is a question I frequently ask. It's a question I imagine she asked. *What does love require me to do?*

Love prompts us to act, to get involved. Love isn't passive, sitting on the sidelines, trusting someone else will make things right. It jumps right in and starts serving. It rises, comes near, helps out.

Sometimes love will require a listening ear. I think about our daughter Jade and how she comes alive during one-on-one time. She's never the one to need big events or busy agendas. Just an hour, a quiet conversation, someone who cares.

Sometimes love will require us to share our resources with someone who needs them. Our children often have to sort out a system for sharing when they play because there are always more bodies than there are bikes/skateboards/balls/pool floaties/game pieces/whatever. We could just buy more, but where would the lesson be in that? I like knowing that as they learn to consider their sisters and brothers here at home, they are learning how to consider the people they'll come across after they leave.

Sometimes love will require a kind word to be spoken. Not long ago, a friend of mine was going through a great challenge with her adult son, who was making decisions for his life that seemed terribly out of character. I knew her heart was hurting, and I made a point of texting to tell her I was praying for her. Friends often do the same for me, and it lifts my spirits every time.

Sometimes love will require including someone who has been left out. For many years now, my family has known that whenever I can get them all in the same room, I'm absolutely going to dress them alike. One time it was bright-yellow dresses for the girls and me and, for the guys, these gold-and-black V-neck shirts that were supposed to look like an intricate African print but wound up looking like an abstract painting gone wrong. Another time we all wore reds and shades of burgundy, with black tights and boots for the girls and me and black pants for all the guys. This past Christmas, we all did a black-and-white buffalo check, with a little gray thrown in for fun.

I'm not very active on social media—how people have the time I'll never know—but Tony keeps his Twitter feed up-to-date, proof that at least once a month . . . and sometimes once a week . . . the Dungy crew is dressed alike. Whether it's one of the children's birthday dinners, Mother's Day or Father's Day, Thanksgiving or Christmas, or someone's graduation ceremony, there I am buzzing through Target or Men's Wearhouse, praying they have the sizes I need. The older kids sometimes pull out the eye roll, but I have to tell you, when I underreact to this gesture, they come circling back every time. "Okay, fine. I'll be in the picture, Mom. What do I have to wear?"

I think we call this reverse psychology. I'm pretty good at it, if I do say so myself.

Here's why the family outfits are so important to me: I want everyone in our household to know they're seen, they're loved, and they are absolutely one of us. And I do mean *household* here—as in the ancient, biblical sense.

In times past, a household didn't include only the people who lived in your house. A household—sometimes called a *household of faith*—comprised the parents and children, any extended family who were present, neighbors who might be paying a visit, and strangers who were passing through. Sounds like a party to me!

My interpretation of this little detail from history is that if you are in our home when it's picture time, then you get dressed in a Team Dungy outfit. You are officially part of the team.

I've had more than a few people tell me over the years that they went online to look for a family picture of us and came away totally and thoroughly confused. "Every picture I looked at featured a whole different array of kids!" they say. "Who's who? Who's yours? *How* many kids do you have?"

I just laugh.

By this point, on any given day, our family portraits could have featured sixty or seventy different souls. There's Tony and me. There are our first three children. There are our adopted children. There are countless children who were grafted in through foster care. On a few occasions, our kids had friends over, and they got dressed and photographed too.

I wouldn't have it any other way.

When you're here, you're one of us. We see you. We love you. You're in.

. . .

Here's another one: sometimes love will require meaningful touch. For so many of the kids who come through our home, physical touch has been a negative thing. Children are incredibly vulnerable, and for some parents or caregivers who are stressed and upset, lashing out at their children is a temptation they often indulge. It's devastating to see a child who has been harmed physically. Like a frightened kitten, they cower at the slightest movement, they keep a great distance from some adults, and they live in constant terror that they'll be harmed again.

Our little guy Juewel was like that. He came to our home when he was six years old, and while I could tell that he was a sweet boy, he was very shy, mousy, and withdrawn. He'd keep his little head down, cutting his eyes upward to see where he was going. From the beginning, he was more comfortable with me than he was with Tony. He steered clear of Tony for some time, unsure of how this male authority figure was going to act. He'd seen a lot. He'd been through a lot. He was taking zero chances here.

Over time, Juewel saw that Tony was as steady as they come. You could almost see his little brain processing the trend: *Hey, this man doesn't yell at me. He doesn't spank me. He never slams his fist down on the table. He never throws things against the wall.*

He uses his hands to hug me, not harm me. I think I could trust this man.

During the first few days that we had Juewel, Tony confided in his friend James Brown during one of their weekly online Bible studies that we really needed prayer for this boy. Tony explained that Juewel had been in an abusive home and was untrusting of him, and so the two men began to pray that Juewel would be able to trust each person in our home and that he would know he was safe with us. James came to our house not long after and was absolutely stunned when Juewel ran up to him, jumped into his lap, and threw his arms around ole J. B. "*This* is the young man we've been praying for?" James said with a big laugh.

There wasn't a dry eye among us adults. We knew our boy had turned the corner. He was safe. He was happy. He felt loved.

On the day that we got to take Juewel to the local courthouse and have his name officially changed to Dungy, I thought his smile could light a thousand suns. "When I go to school tomorrow," he said, "I get to write Juewel *Dungy*. I'm part of the family now!"

. . .

It's a profound thing, realizing we're not alone in this big world. To know that we belong—that someone really does see us and care—is a deeply meaningful gift. When I daydream, my visions are of every child on the planet being placed in a healthy, stable forever home. I can get myself so worked up over this image of every child being set up for success that I cry. I can *see* it. I can *feel* it. I just know that this goal can be reached.

Toward the end of 2021, Tony and I began fostering three more children—a nine-year-old and two little ones under the age of two. They are just fantastic. We're still hip deep in all the logistics and meetings and appointments that have to happen . . . some of their needs are profound. But those things will get worked out, I know. For now, I'm just focused on them.

I'm just focused on what love requires.

That's the choice that precedes every other worthwhile choice, the choice to faithfully and thoroughly love.

ACKNOWLEDGMENTS

We are grateful to the team at Tyndale House Publishers—especially Linda Howard and Danika King—for their enthusiastic and expert championing of this project; to our literary agent, D. J. Snell, for his ever-present support and prayers; and to Ashley Wiersma, whose masterful touch helped us condense our thoughts into an orderly story. We were richly blessed from start to finish with project partners who both believed in this message and were committed to helping us communicate it well.

ABOUT THE AUTHORS

Lauren Dungy is an early childhood specialist and a bestselling children's book author who serves as vice president of the Dungy Family Foundation, which helps meet the spiritual, social, and educational needs of those in her community. She both partners with several organizations in the Tampa area to advocate for foster care and adoption and is involved in many charitable causes centering on education and Christian outreach. The Dungys are the parents of eleven children.

Tony Dungy is a #1 *New York Times* bestselling author whose books include *Quiet Strength*, *Uncommon*, *The Mentor Leader*, and *Uncommon Marriage*. He led the Indianapolis Colts to Super Bowl victory on February 4, 2007, the first such win for an African American head coach. Tony established another NFL first by becoming the first head coach to lead his teams to the playoffs for ten consecutive years. He joined the Colts in 2002 after serving as the most successful head coach in Tampa Bay Buccaneers history. Tony has also held assistant coaching positions with the University of Minnesota, Pittsburgh Steelers, Kansas City Chiefs, and Minnesota Vikings. Before becoming a coach, he played three seasons in the NFL. Tony was inducted into the Pro Football Hall of Fame in 2016.

Tony has been involved in a wide variety of charitable organizations, including All Pro Dad, Abe Brown Ministries, Fellowship of Christian Athletes, Athletes in Action, Mentors for Life, Big Brothers Big Sisters, and Boys & Girls Clubs. He has also worked with Basket of Hope, Impact for Living, the Black Coaches Association National Convention, Indiana Black Expo, the United Way of Central Indiana, and the American Diabetes Association. He retired from coaching in 2009 and now serves as a studio analyst for NBC's *Football Night in America*. Tony and his wife, Lauren, are the parents of eleven children.

NOTES

INTRODUCTION
1. Richard Allen Farmer, *Caressing the Creed: Reflections on the Apostles' Creed* (Bloomington, IN: WestBow Press, 2016), 49.

2: AGAINST THE GRAIN
1. James Mills, "Why Does Jim Carrey Wish We Were All Rich & Famous?," Lighthouse International Group (2021), https://www.legends.report/why-does -jim-carrey-wish-we-were-all-rich-famous/.
2. *Merriam-Webster*, s.v. "integrity (n.)," accessed November 5, 2021, https://www .merriam-webster.com/dictionary/integrity.
3. "Benedict's 12-Step Guide to Humility," *Christianity Today*, August 8, 2008, https://www.christianitytoday.com/history/2008/august/benedicts-12-step-guide -to-humility.html.

3: "LEAD ME, LORD"
1. Priscilla Shirer, *He Speaks to Me: Preparing to Hear from God* (Chicago: Moody, 2006), 157.

6: "WE" OVER "I"
1. *Merriam-Webster*, s.v. "selfless (adj.)," accessed January 20, 2022, https://www .merriam-webster.com/dictionary/selfless.
2. *Merriam-Webster*, s.v. "consider (v.)," accessed January 20, 2022, https://www .merriam-webster.com/dictionary/consider.

10: FULL SURRENDER
1. Augustine, *Confessions* 1.1.

CHANGING THE LIVES OF CHILDREN
IN POVERTY THROUGH SPONSORSHIP

Imagine being able to change a child's life from one of hardship and loneliness to one of hope and meaning.

Compassion International is a child sponsorship organization that works with more than 8,000 frontline church partners in countries around the world to deliver its holistic child development program. Tyndale and Compassion are committed to releasing children from poverty in Jesus' name through this proven model of one-to-one sponsorship.

Sponsoring a child through Compassion allows you to follow your child's growth as he or she is nurtured to health, educated, and exposed to the hope of the gospel.

YOUR LOVE FOR ONE ANOTHER WILL PROVE TO THE WORLD THAT YOU ARE MY DISCIPLES. —JOHN 13:35

Releasing children from poverty
Compassion
in Jesus' name

SPONSOR A CHILD TODAY!
VISIT COMPASSION.COM

CP1473

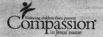

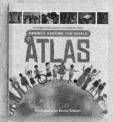 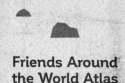

Tony and Lauren Dungy bring together their faith, love of children, and love of sports to tell stories of inspiration and encouragement.

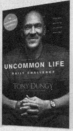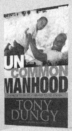

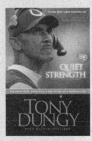
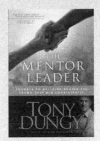
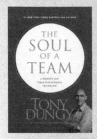
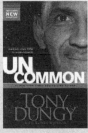

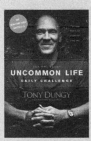

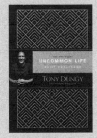

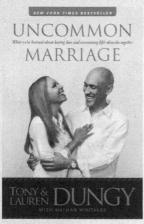
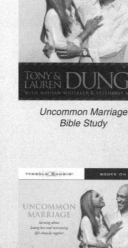
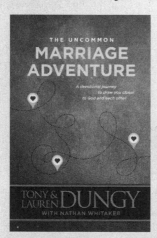

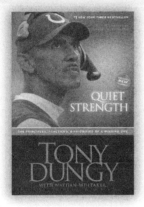
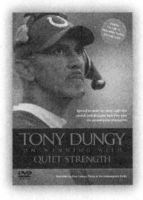
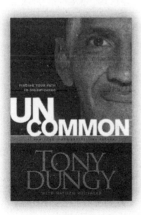

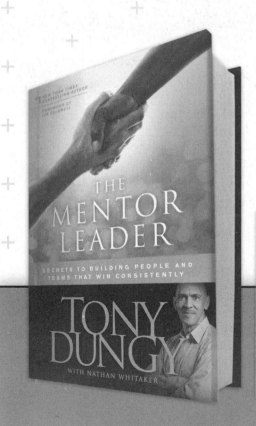
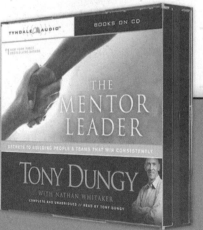